Tempus ORAL HISTORY *Series*

Witham
voices

Jack and Ida Cunningham at their wedding.

Tempus ORAL HISTORY *Series*

Witham
voices

Compiled by
Mary Flynn and Diane Watson

TEMPUS

First published 2000
Copyright © Mary Flynn and Diane Watson, 2000

Tempus Publishing Limited
The Mill, Brimscombe Port,
Stroud, Gloucestershire, GL5 2QG

ISBN 0 7524 1854 8

Typesetting and origination by
Tempus Publishing Limited
Printed in Great Britain by
Midway Clark Printing, Wiltshire

The age of horse power.

Contents

Witham football team in the grounds of The Grove.

Vote for STRUTT.
Your Old Member and your Old Friend.
"OLD FRIENDS ARE BEST."
Photo by H. Hall.

"A motto old and hard to beat:
An Essex Man for an Essex Seat."

VOTE FOR **STRUTT**

Who is an Essex Man,
Who lives amongst you,
Who knows your interests.

IS YOUR OLD MEMBER
AND YOUR OLD FRIEND.

VOTE FOR **STRUTT**
The Popular Candidate.

VOTE FOR **STRUTT**
The Working Man's Friend.

"STRAIGHT AND TRUE."

Printed and Published by Shearcroft & Hawkes, Braintree.

Vote for Strutt.

The Infants' School, Chipping Hill, April 1939.

Introduction

Witham, which lies twelve miles south of Colchester, has progressed during the last hundred years from a small, rural market community to the present thriving commercial and commuter town. Fortunately, much of the main street and Chipping Hill has retained its character. The merchandise in the High Street shops, from mangles to tumble driers and from chalk and slates to computers, has changed many times over the years, but the vivid characters who presided over these establishments left a deep impression on all their customers. We regret the passing of such eccentrics and wish we had encountered them first hand.

The many public houses in Witham had their fair share of colourful hosts and clients. Although one or two of these inns have disappeared, the majority, such as the Red Lion, the White Hart, the Spread Eagle and the Wheatsheaf still retain much of their old charm.

The River Brain flows gently through the centre of the town. It figured largely in the memories of our contributors and still affords an equal pleasure today. The countryside around Witham sustained several farms which featured regularly in the lives of the townspeople. They recall working and playing on Cox's, Freebournes and Cuppers Farms, to mention just three.

The railway has always been of major importance. At one time Witham was a busy junction for moving livestock and freight; now its main task is carrying hundreds of people daily to work and back. Many of those who were part of this transformation have been kind enough to share their memories with us, both humorous and serious.

Lucy Croxall and the Girls' Training Corps.

So many of the people we interviewed, now in their eighties and nineties, have known each other from childhood. They attended the same schools – the Board School in Maldon Road, the Church School in Guithavon Street and the little school in Chipping Hill. Though their lives took different directions, many remained in Witham and maintained those early friendships.

Our contributors have generously lent us some 120 photographs and documents. We would like to thank all those who have given their invaluable assistance to the compilation of this book, especially Mr Fred Gaymer and Mr Percy Adams for access to their extensive records and Mr Albert Poulter, local historian, for his advice.

This has been an enjoyable experience for us. We feel privileged to have met such diverse characters, most of whom we now regard as friends. We are grateful for the gallons of tea and coffee supplied, the chuckles and the chat, but mainly for the knowledge we have gained. It has been exciting to travel back in time and see Witham through earlier eyes. The Avenue no longer appears as just a thoroughfare, but crowded with children playing in the trees and courting couples embracing beneath them. In fact, now, wherever we walk in the town, we can conjure up its distinctive past.

It has been a truly fascinating journey through the decades in the company of these Witham folk.

Mary Flynn & Diane Watson
December 1999

CHAPTER 1
Home Life

Fred Gaymer's parents at Cuppers Farm.

Spiders at the Dairy

When I was about five years old, my brother was sent out early in the mornings to collect skimmed milk, which was very cheap, from Freebournes Farm. I often went with him and we had to get up very early to be at the entrance to the farm by about seven o'clock. Several boys and sometimes a few grown-ups waited for the farm foreman to go to the dairy and skim the cream off the pans of milk; he then sold us the skimmed milk. We were not allowed to pass the entrance to the farmyard or go to the dairy until we had been called. It was first come, first served, and sometimes there was not enough skimmed milk to supply all those waiting. When I was older I was sent on my own. I remember waiting near the low building next to the entrance. There was always a lot of large spider webs under the eaves and the taller boys caught flies and put them in the webs.

Fred Gaymer

The dovecote at Lodge Farm.

Chicken for Christmas

Like most people we knew, we had a few chickens in the back garden but Christmas was the only time we ate one. Two were killed, one for my grandmother in London and one for us. Every year after the war we travelled by train to London and enjoyed a big family Christmas. As an only child I was very excited and always looked forward to spending the holidays with lots of young cousins.

Shirley Harper

Lodge Farm

I was born in 1917 at Lodge Farm, opposite where Lynfields Garage is now. It was rented

then from Phil Wheaton. It was overrun with rats at the farm and my mother, who was very particular, couldn't stand it. I remember the old dovecote in the grounds.

Percy Adams

Christmas House

My father was born in Chipping Hill and I was born down the Maldon Road, opposite where Crofters wine bar is now, in 1909. My aunt, Mrs Chaplin, lived in the Christmas House for a time. My father was a Liberal and an avid reader of the newspapers. I still have copies which he kept of the *Nuneaton Observer* dated October 26th 1917, which cost 1d, *The Midland Daily Telegraph* dated

October 27th 1917, then the *Sunday Dispatch* from 1953 at 2½d and the *Daily Mail* of 1955 at 1½d – these are over forty years old now.

Vera Howell

Black and White TV

We had a little nine-inch television set in the fifties and neighbours who hadn't yet bought one often came in to watch it with us. That was quite a normal thing to do then. The house was full when the Coronation was broadcast. I remember everyone crammed indoors when outside it was a lovely sunny day. I watched *The Quatermass Experiment* which was exciting. I also remember *The Appleyards*, *Dixon of Dock Green* and *Café Continental*. As a child I liked *Muffin the Mule*.

Ken Smith

A Country Lane

I was born in a little terraced cottage at the top of Church Street in 1921. The rest of Church Street was a country lane that led to the Cherry Tree Crossing where my grandmother, Mrs Beatrice Dennis, was the crossing keeper. She lived there with her second husband, who was a plate-layer. My father was one of twenty-two children which included four sets of twins; unfortunately only thirteen survived. The house wasn't big enough for everybody and some of the children had to be boarded out to local families. My father went to the family who ran the Cricketers at Goldhanger and they unofficially raised him.

Dennis Johnson

Beattie and Ub

My mother Beattie Lane married my father Ub Smith in St Nicholas' church on Bonfire Night 1939. She wore orange blossom in her hair and carried a bouquet of carnations. They lived for a while in a rented bungalow in Maldon Road. When my father enlisted in the Army my mother temporarily left Witham to live with her parents in St Osyth.

Diane Watson

Ub and Beattie Smith's wedding at St Nicholas' church in 1939.

Cuppers Farm in later years.

Cuppers

I was born on 15 April 1907, down Maldon Road in Park Cottages. They are no longer there. The filling station bought the site and knocked the three houses down, even though they were not condemned. They were nice little brick houses, too. My father was an estate carpenter who worked on Freebournes Estate and then after the First World War he took on fifteen acres here and we farmed it as a smallholding. This is where I was brought up.

Fred Gaymer

Buffalo Row

They pulled the bungalows down in 1939; they said they weren't high enough. They were beautiful little cottages and very warm; they must have been there a hundred years, easily. We had an open coal fire for the warmth – it was lovely – and what you called a kitchen range for the cooking. We paid in a club for the coal: we paid all year, then bought the coal for about 1s a hundredweight.

Connie Edwards

Miss Hunt's Private Home

Miss Hunt was what I would call a very homely woman, between thirty and forty years old. Her father was a Minister with the Church of England in Feering. She took in five or six homeless children and she made it into a real home for them – they were like a family. Miss Hunt fostered them but wouldn't take anyone older than seven years. The Private Home, as it was known, was where Barclays Bank is today.

Vera Howell

Guithavon Road

We lived at 19 Guithavon Road in 1958. We bought it for £725, I think, and we sold it in 1967 for £2,850. Of course, we had made a lot of improvements as well as doing a lot of work to it.

Ken Thompson

Three Holer

Only a few houses in the town had the sort of toilets we know today. Houses and cottages just outside the town had a little house at the bottom of the garden called a pail closet. There was no chain to pull, as there was no water pipes or taps. Some houses had a three-holer where you could sit side by side over a cesspit.

Fred Gaymer

Collection

Millbridge Road was all allotments up from the river to the corner of Hatfield Road where the fire station is. I used to collect the rents as the allotments were owned by Lord Rayleigh. It wasn't much, probably half a crown a year. They built the fire and ambulance stations first and the flats later.

Percy Adams

The Front Parlour

I recall my grandparents' house, Ferndale, in Rickstones Road. The front parlour was sacrosanct. We never sat in there. There were large framed pictures on the walls, 'The Stag at Bay' and a Victorian girl at prayer. The furniture shone with polish and in the window was an aspidistra. The table was covered with a velvet cloth and the family Bible was always open at the day's reading.

Diane Watson

George and Cecilia Smith at Ferndale.

Dennis Johnson's grandfather, Samuel.

shilling. I had to work very hard for this, like most other children then. My jobs were to wash up, clean the brass knobs on the kitchen cupboard, black-lead the range and cardinal-red the kitchen floor.

Shirley Harper

May Wedding

I married the local policeman's daughter, Mary Howe, at St Nicholas' church in 1960. It was a beautiful, sunny day in May and as we walked to church all the may trees were in full blossom. We were married by the Revd Everett who came from Kelvedon, as Revd Black, the Witham vicar, was on holiday that week. We had our wedding reception at the Spread Eagle.

John Hollick

Rainwater

We had to dip our water for drinking, cooking and washing from a well. This was always nice, cold water to drink, but not so good for washing as it was hard water and you had to use a lot of soap and soda. We collected as much rainwater as we could, off the roofs of buildings, and stored it in tanks or water butts – this was much better for washing.

Fred Gaymer

Bricks and Mortar

Pete and I bought our first house in Albert Road for £2,300. Our mortgage was about £12 a month. We sold that house for £3,500 and bought a detached bungalow for £4,000; we then moved to St Nicholas' Drive – the house there cost £5,500.

Margaret Brannan

65 Cressing Road

My father Albert and uncle Victor were in reserved occupations at Crittall's and I have lived at 65 Cressing Road from 1939, when I was about a year old. We had a cooking range in the kitchen which also

Pocket Money

My dad gave me a shilling a week pocket money and my mum paid me another heated the home. I remember the fogs: they were so thick that people would sometimes pass their own homes. When I was young you could name everyone in Cressing Road. That was before they built the school and Templars Estate in the open fields which lay between our house and Rivenhall.

Mick Horsley

Timber-framed Dwelling

I got married in 1930 and built a bungalow near Blunts Hall Road railway arch. I built that afore I was married – I built the majority of it, it was a timber-framed dwelling. It took a couple of years and the cost was under £200.

Fred Gaymer

Journey into Space

Our parents didn't have to call us in when we were playing in the street after tea. As soon as we heard the theme tune to *Dick Barton, Special Agent* all the kids would disappear into their homes to hear the wireless. I also remember listening to *Journey into Space*, which was about space travel, which just seemed too fantastic to imagine then. We all gathered round the wireless and sat there enthralled.

Shirley Harper

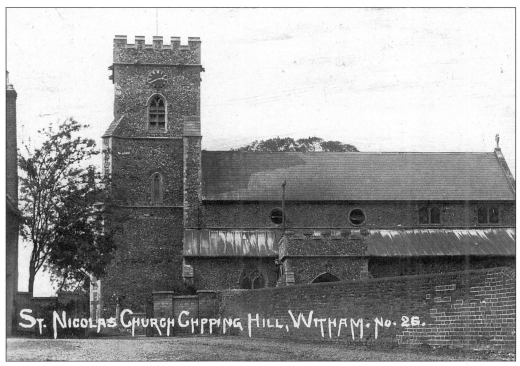

St Nicholas' church, Chipping Hill.

Lodge Farm, where Percy Adams was born in 1917.

Mrs Cunningham

I lived with my future mother-in-law up Church Street. She had three sons; they were all in the Forces during the war. When my boyfriend Jack and his brothers returned, we married and eventually moved into a house quite near. We had a gap of ten years between our second and third son so we took in lots of foster children. One, a new-born baby girl, we adopted.

Ida Cunningham

Cow Shed

Where my father lived when he was growing up there was a front door on one side of the room and the back door on the other. When you went out the back door you stepped straight into the cow shed. When father got up in the morning he would let the dog out and while he boiled the kettle and had a cup of tea the dog would herd the cows into the milking shed from the fields.

Percy Adams

Weekly Wash

Although my mother never used the local laundries, she did have a woman in to help with the weekly wash. The whole family's wash was done on the one day.

Vera Howell

Tiptoe Home

After dances at the Public Hall, we would walk home quietly so as not to wake up the street. Witham was a small place, everyone knew everyone, so we had to be quiet or they would tell our parents and we'd be in trouble.

John Ashcroft

Street Lighting

The first street lighting was by gas lamps. I remember a Mr Perry, who was called the lamplighter, walking round the town lighting the lamps. He carried a long pole with a metal hook at the top for pulling the chain to turn the gas on; also on the pole was a small flame for lighting the gas. Later these lamps were improved by having a small pilot light which was lit all the time, and when the chain was pulled the lamp automatically lit. Late at night the lamplighter had to go round again and put the lights out.

Fred Gaymer

Hopscotch in the Street

Just after the war, as a youngster, I would play hopscotch in the middle of Cressing Road. There was very little traffic. The bread roundsman who worked for Witham Co-op made his deliveries by horse and cart up until 1950. I sometimes rode on the cart – the bags of flour were stacked under the seat.

Mick Horsley

Opposite the Library

We rented our first home at Freebournes Farm, opposite the present Witham Library, from Mr Philip Wheaton the farmer. We used what is now the chip shop as our front room. I suppose we stayed there for about two years.

John Hollick

Treat Yourself

My mother used to speak about life before the National Health Service, when people paid to visit their doctor. She remembered that if you felt ill you mostly treated yourself. The most popular remedies were Epsom Salts and Beechams Pills.

Diane Watson

The Dentist

In 1916, when I was about seven, we moved into a house in the High Street, where Newland Court is now, you know, where the flats are. There was quite a biggish house there and some days part of it was used by Mr King the dentist. He came over from Chelmsford. There was a

Batsford Hotel (on the left), Newland Street.

connecting door and my mother cleaned his rooms for him. The people waited to see Mr King in our sitting room. He paid a separate rent for the rooms and we got our treatment free.

Vera Howell

Boot Scraper

During the winter and rainy weather the roads and paths were often muddy, and most houses had a boot scraper fixed near the front door. Batsford Hotel in Newland Street still has one which must have been there a great many years. You can see that it was well used as it is worn in places and misshapen.

Fred Gaymer

21 Maldon Road

Before I was married I bought a house at 21 Maldon Road for £200. It was occupied by an elderly brother and sister, Mr and Miss Capon. They remained there until they decided it was time for them to move to an old folks' bungalow. My wife and I then moved in.

John Hollick

Suet Pudding

Dinner in the middle of the day was usually suet pudding, vegetables, gravy and not too much meat. For supper we often had bread and butter but sometimes there was cake or buns.

Bert Baxter

Gates and Fences

All front gardens and the entrances to the back of houses, shops and businesses had fences and gates because cattle, sheep and pigs were often driven along the roads to the slaughterhouse. When people saw livestock coming they went into shops or into people's gardens, behind the gates, to feel safer and get out of the way.

Fred Gaymer

Big Dishes

When Pop was on the butcher's round he had a lot of vegetables given to him. He and his sons literally ate like horses – they had big meat dishes and, I'm not kidding, they were full and flowing over. Jack, my husband, and the younger son, Ken, worked with their dad, Ted, in the slaughterhouse. The other son, Les, was apprenticed to the tailor in the High Street, Mr Taylor.

Ida Cunningham

Annie Stock

My mother, Annie Stock, was born and bred in Witham. She was one of five daughters. She lived in various houses in Witham, including a cottage opposite Park Stores where the car park is now. My mother liked to go out for a drink and we often went to the George pub in the evening.

John Hollick

Braintree Road, Witham.

19

Foresters Health Insurance

It was about 2s 6d for a bottle of medicine when The Foresters used to manage the health insurance. It all got took away from them and the Government then set up offices similar to what they have now.

Fred Gaymer

Prefabs

The prefabs in Church Street were an American design. They had two bedrooms, a large living room and a kitchen, as well as a bathroom. It was all electric and we had a fridge provided for another 2s 6d a week. The 29s a week rent included a big garden and storage shed. We were there about two years.

Pat Smith

Rag Rugs

If you were lucky you had a bit of lino. Most had mats, rugs made out of rags which you hooked through sacking. We had a little coal fire for heating in the living room. There were fireplaces in all the rooms but really we couldn't use them because coal cost too much.

Rose Willshire

Paraffin at a Shilling a Can

Years ago, to start with it was oil lamps. You could either have single or double burners. We bought the paraffin oil at Mondy's or the Co-op – I think it cost about a shilling a can.

Most people had a double burner if they could afford it.

Reg Edwards

Lord Rayleigh

Lord Rayleigh used to own the timber-framed buildings in Bridge Street that were joined onto the side of the old Morning Star. The Almshouses belonged to the Church and every Christmas they were given 5cwt of coal paid for by the Church. The present Bridge Hospital has served different purposes in its history, including being the Eastern Counties Industrial School, whose stone inscription still remains in the cornice above the entrance arch – it has somehow been concealed.

Percy Adams

Boarders

I got married in 1935 when I was twenty-six years old; my husband came from Sheringham. Sadly he died in the Masonic Hospital when our son was eight years old and our baby daughter eighteen months old. We had just moved into a new house in Highfields Road when my husband died. I took in boarders at 15s a week. One was a Chipping Hill School teacher, and we are still friendly to this day.

Vera Howell

Royal Wedding

On the present Queen's wedding day, my son Colin was born. Sister Hinds, who lived

Fred and Rose Willshire's wedding group.

in the bungalow in Collingwood Road, was furious with me. I hadn't got a wireless in the bedroom, so she could hear the wedding. I said, 'To hell with royalty!'

Ida Cunningham

Prisoners' Meals

As the wife of Witham's Police Inspector in the sixties, it was my responsibility to provide meals for the prisoners. It always had to be mashed potatoes, as they weren't allowed to use a knife, ham or corned beef and perhaps a tin of peas – they could eat this with a fork or spoon. I made cheese or egg sandwiches for their tea – it was often eggs as we kept chickens at the police station. Cornflakes for breakfast and several pots of tea a day. As we lived on the premises they used our

china and I had an allowance of 1s 6d per person per meal.

Sylma Shayshutt

Mrs Tucker

I had piano lessons from Mrs Tucker. She lived in Braintree Road and charged 7s 6d a term. Mrs Tucker took me to the Salvation Army at Chelmsford where I played the piano and accompanied her husband who played the xylophone and sang.

Daphne LeSage

Bridal Dress

I was married in St Nicholas' church on 29 April 1947, in a lovely dress which cost

Jack and Ida Cunningham's wedding party.

19s 11d from Denny's in Moulsham Street. I believe it was rayon; of course, I didn't have a lot of make-up, just a dab of talcum powder.

Ida Cunningham

How Electricity Came

My father being estate carpenter, he helped wire several different houses in Witham, including Freebournes, and I remember working at The Grove when they first had electricity. They used to have an engine which drove a dynamo. There were large seals all round in the little building. That's how electricity first came about in Witham. My dad done the carpentry side and worked with Ernie Woodwards.

Fred Gaymer

Funeral Hat

My father's funeral hat always had to be brushed in a certain way. If we were lucky he allowed us to brush it for him. The highly polished hand bier which was used at the time was hired from Moores in Kelvedon.

Daphne LeSage

Highfields Farm

The Highfields Farm had what they called a running pump which never stopped. We also had one up the road where I used to live when I was a boy. On wash day you filled the copper, you filled the bath, filled the buckets, in fact everything you could use, you filled. People had a bath every week, either Friday or Saturday night. It was a tin bath in those days.

Reg Edwards

Old Tin Bath

When we moved to this house we still brought the old tin bath in and bathed in the living room in front of the open fire. Although there was some electricity in the house, the wash house outside still had a gas lamp.

Fred Willshire

The Crispy Bit

Mother would put the nice crispy bit of the meat on Dad's plate. I would have liked it occasionally but the man of the house and the breadwinner always had the best bit and was served first. Teatime was always about five o'clock and you had to be back for it or you would be in trouble. At night you had to be in by ten o'clock: Dad locked the door for the night then and if you were late, hard luck! I remember my eldest brother got locked out and we had to throw the key out to him. Sometimes my mother would slide down with a key for a latecomer.

Ken Smith

Sparrow Pie

We used to prop a couple of bricks up with sticks that had been attached to string. We would sprinkle some crumbs and then sit quietly and wait, then give a quick tug on the string while the birds were feeding. We soon had enough for a sparrow pie. We'd just flay the breast and put it in a pie or a suet pudding. It was very tender and a real luxury.

Ida Cunningham

Water Tower

The water was pumped from a spring into the water tower in Collingwood Road, then piped into the mains system. There weren't many mains really in those days: for instance in Mill Lane there was a line of houses and there was only one tap outside for all those houses to use.

Fred Gaymer

117 Cressing Road

I was born at No. 117 Cressing Road in the summer of 1928. My father worked at

Ken Smith's mother outside No. 29 Church Street.

23

Crittall's and had a smallholding in Guithavon Street where the car park is now. He had big greenhouses – you can still see the white lines on the wall where the greenhouses had been attached. He also kept some pigs.

Eileen Smith

Rates at £19 a Year

We started off our married life in a brick cottage on the corner of Guithavon Road. When this was condemned and pulled down we moved to our present house in March 1958. We could have had a council house but the rent was higher than the mortgage repayments and would have cost more than the £750 we paid to buy this house. Our mortgage was £1 14s 4d a month and the rates were £19 a year.

Rose Willshire

It Wasn't Cheerful

I remember having an abscess as big as a duck's egg just below the heart. Dr Ted Gimson came and lanced it; he used lots of wadding. It wasn't cheerful! Then Mother said, 'How much do I owe you?' Dr Gimson said, 'I will send the bill in.' He never did, of course: he was that sort of man.

Albert Poulter

Fenced In

The Green in the middle of the houses used to have an iron fence around it. I could pop the children inside and they were there all day long. I fetched 'em when there was a meal ready. Then they took the railings for the war effort and we couldn't do that any more.

Connie Edwards

Sewerage

They eventually put drainage up Blunts Hall Road and my father, who was living at Cuppers Cottage and owned the land from the house down towards Spinks Lane, had to contribute to these costs.

Fred Gaymer

Three Lights and a Plug

When these houses were connected to the power supply the electricity company installed three lights and a plug if you paid a quarter in advance – that was 12s 6d. You had to pay that every quarter whether you used any electricity or not.

Reg Edwards

CHAPTER 2

School Years

A recent photograph of Reg and Connie Edwards.

Bicycle Made for Two

We've been married sixty-three years now. Reg used to pick me up and take me to school, giving me a ride on the crossbar of his bike when I was only five years old. So really you might as well say we've been together all our lives!

Connie Edwards

Break of Dawn

The six weeks of the school summer holidays – well, that was for pea picking and potato picking. I set off with my mother at the break of dawn; we probably had to go to four or five farms before we could get any work.

Percy Adams

Maldon Road Infants' School sports day in the fifties.

Miss Gentry's Strawberries

When I was four and a half years old, I attended the Church School. My first teacher was Miss Gentry, who had a smallholding in Tiptree. she would bring us in strawberries and during the war this was really special.

Mick Horsley

Headmistress

In 1954 I came to Witham to take over the Infants' School in Maldon Road. I had previously taught in Egypt for three years and then in Southend. Templars School was built and our junior pupils transferred there. I taught the elder pupils and Miss French took the smaller ones. They were mixed classes and I aimed for them all to read and write and use numbers quite well before they moved up to the Junior School. Later we grew to three classes and then Howbridge Infants' was built.

Grace Rose

Open Churches

When I was at the Church School in Guithavon Street we went to the church which was next door once a week for morning assembly. I can remember going into the church to play with a group of friends after school – the doors were never kept locked in those days, of course. One day when we were playing houses in amongst the pews, Miss Lucy Croxall came in and nabbed us. I was the slowest to get away and she caught me.

Angela Dursley

Piano Lessons

Well, I went to the Maldon Road school. The master when I first started was Mr Quick. I had piano lessons from him – I suppose I was about four and a half – and I remember that Mr Quick was strict but nice. We had a piano in our front room which I practised on. After I was married my husband bought me a new one which is still in my family.

Vera Howell

Christmas Orange

The Vicar came to the school and gave us all an orange for Christmas.

Percy Adams

School Matches

I learnt more from Miss Welland, the headmistress, than any other teacher I ever had. I played in the football team but we had to practise in the local park as there was no pitch at the school. In February 1949 we played a match at Silver End School, which we lost. I don't remember the name of the teacher who accompanied us, but I can recall the team, most of whom still live and work in Witham. They are Timothy Collard, Michael Bailey, Ronnie Bendall, Luther Game, Keith Brown, Leonard Rushen, Ernest Willshire, Ronald Hawkes, Michael (Mick) Horsley, Roy Slater and Roy Shelley.

Mick Horsley

The Church School football team in February 1949.

Church School, Guithavon Street.

Music Teachers

When I was at Witham Secondary Modern, Miss Lucy Croxall taught music. She was a bit eccentric and she had a catchphrase: 'Did I hear a whisper?', which was said very sharply. Mr Brett also taught music. I remember him as a quiet man.

Ken Smith

Vicarage Meadow

The Church School and also the Infants' School at Chipping Hill used to have outings on the Vicarage Meadow – races for the children followed by warm tea, buns and that sort of thing. I remember one year I won two races. I only got one prize, though: when I went to get the second one, they said, 'Oh no, you can't have two prizes.' I think either the Miss Luards or Miss Pattison were giving out the prizes that year,

and even after all this time I feel I should have been given that prize. I think they were spinsters – they hadn't used the Avenue to do any courting, had they?

Fred Gaymer

Over the Handlebars

I remember during the war, we all had to take a gas mask with us to school. One day while I was cycling, mine got caught between my knees and I went head-first over the handlebars in Braintree Road.

John Ashcroft

Church School

The girls were on one side and the boys on the other. When we went in the Infants' we were on the girls' side to start with. I was four and a half years old and when I got to be five was moved round to the other side to be with the boys. On Empire Day there was a big parade, with the boys gathered in the road and the girls at the side. They marched to church with the boys going in the east door and the girls in the other one. I didn't mind, it made a change, and after twelve o'clock we were given the rest of the day off.

Percy Adams

Mr Ashton

After the war there was a shortage of teachers and the authorities arranged short training courses for returning servicemen. I particularly remember Mr Ashton, who taught me at junior school and later transferred to senior school.

Mick Horsley

Maldon Road School Strike

In 1922 the master at the Maldon Road School was Mr Portass. One day, one of the boys had done something wrong – it was about an inkwell I think. The master pushed him to the floor in the cloakroom; the floor was all stone then and he caught his face on the stone. Well, his face was covered in blood and we all screamed. We went to see Captain Shafto Abrey and he called a School Board meeting. The outcome was that we all decided on a strike and so Mr Portass was moved to another position the next day. We then had a Mr Hyde as a master – he was a very nice man.

Vera Howell

Left School Three Times

I left school on my fourteenth birthday. I'd felt I should go to work as soon as possible to help my mother. That was the first time, but the authorities made me return until the end of the term, when I left for the second time. I left school again for the third time when I was ninety. I had been asked to return and talk to the children when I was seventy-five and did so for the next fifteen years.

Albert Poulter

School Meals

School meals were cooked at the kitchens in Bramston School, put into hot food containers and delivered to other local

Albert Poulter as a child.

schools. The meals were reasonably priced and most of the children had school dinners. They also catered for one diabetic child who attended our school and received special food. Also, all the children received a third of a pint of free milk each day.

Grace Rose

Vicarage Picnic

Every now and then during the summer months pupils from the Church School were invited by the Vicar to a picnic at the Vicarage. We all felt very grand sitting and eating in the garden. I remember it with great pleasure.

Angela Dursley

Headmaster Rolls

Mr Rolls was the headmaster and his wife was a teacher. You went in with her when you started, in classes three and four, then you were moved into the other room, which was one big, long room. There must have been near enough a hundred of us, at least seventy or more, anyway. There were two classes, 5A and 5B, and a chap named Mr Crosby was the master. Headmaster Rolls sat up on a platform – he took the oldest of us.

Percy Adams

Gymslip

I normally wore serge frocks to school but I was the first one to wear a school gymslip and blouse. I was really proud when Miss Welland made me stand up in front of the class to show it off.

Hilda Pluck

Mr Crosby

When I went to Witham Secondary Modern School, Mr Crosby, who was an excellent maths teacher, had the back cut out of a gas meter. We could then see it in action and learn how it worked. There was a big gas works in the town, so this information proved useful.

Mick Horsley

Missed Opportunity

Pupils could win a scholarship to go to Braintree High School or to a school in Chelmsford. I passed the arithmetic and geography but missed the start of the second test when I was sent to go and find another girl from Witham who had gone missing. I didn't get the scholarship and although my mother was bitterly disappointed, she didn't make a fuss. In those days you didn't do anything about it.

Vera Howell

Jimmy Knackers

We had teams of three, four, five or even six boys and we would toss up as to which team would bend down against the wall first. The other boys ran and jumped on the back of the first team, forming a sort of pyramid against the school wall. They stayed up there until the other lads admitted defeat and gave in. Then, of course, they changed places and it was the first team's turn to jump. One boy named Turner wore hobnailed boots and was very heavy; I'll never forget his name or his boots! The boys mostly had Blakeys or hobnails.

Albert Poulter

Wintry Days

When I went to the Secondary Modern I caught a bus in the morning from Cressing Road to the town. We walked the rest of the way to school. On wintry days we called in to warm our hands in front of the furnaces at the gasworks.

Mick Horsley

The Local MP

I remember calling in the local MP to show him the state of the school. Actually, the children had to go right down to the bottom of the garden to use the toilets – this was not a good idea, especially in bad weather. They did put wash bowls in the cloakroom. I don't remember the name of the MP but I do remember he had very long arms and waved them around a lot.

Grace Rose

Leaf Houses

At the bottom of the school playing fields there was a wall that backed onto the orchard of a big house. I have lots of good memories of that wall. We climbed over it to scrump the apples from the orchard, we did handstands and practised our two-ball skills against it. In the autumn when the leaves blew over we spent many hours shaping houses from them. We were upset the next morning if the caretaker had raked them up or if the wind had dispersed them.

Angela Dursley

The Cane

Mr Rolls had a cane on his desk and you got hit with it on the hand you didn't use for writing and he gave you another one across your back as you turned. That was very interesting, because the dust used to fly. You had to be very well behaved then, and you must not snitch off the one sitting next to you if you didn't know the answer.

Percy Adams

Displaced Children

Just after the war when I was in the junior school, we had some refugees coming in from Europe. There was a refugee camp at Rivenhall Airfield. Polish children came to school and they told us about their horrendous experiences, but as children we had no conception of their troubles. Looking back now, it was quite sad – this was a small town where we knew everybody and we were unused to strangers. I remember they all wanted to go back to their own country.

Shirley Harper

Sophia Ives, great-grandmother of Dennis Johnson.

Ghost Stories

Mr Maidment, a maths teacher at Witham Secondary Modern, was also a JP. If you missed school he would drop a letter to your parents and because he was a JP they would take notice of it. In his class at one end of the blackboard were multiplication tables which we were expected to be very quick at. He was very strict but sometimes he would take the big Bible out, turn it upside down and then pretend to read a ghost story from it. Suddenly he would slam the Bible shut and get on with the lesson.

Mick Horsley

Sophia Ives

My great grandmother, Mrs Sophia Ives, taught music at Barnardiston House, Chipping Hill. It was a private school and the cost for each child was a penny a day. Barnardiston House is still there and is currently being used as a nursing home for the elderly.

Dennis Johnson

Canon Louard

I lived first of all in the School House next to the school in Maldon Road, and there were two apple trees on the playground edge of the garden. When I had my interview with Canon Louard he asked if I would teach the Ten Commandments. I said, 'No, I will teach Christ's version.' He was disappointed and when I was shown the School House and I asked if the children ever took the apples, he replied rather curtly, 'Thou shalt not steal.'

Grace Rose

Potato Race

I went to Chipping Hill School where Miss Murrells was the head teacher. Another teacher was Miss Griffiths, a Welsh woman. Two fellow pupils come to mind: Kenneth Miller and Margaret Lester. I have always loved sports and one of the best days was when they had races. One of my favourites was the potato race, which entailed lining up ten potatoes, then racing to pick them up one by one and putting them in a bucket. There were three-legged and sack races also, with the winners getting points for their team.

John Hollick

Inkwells

We had inkwells and pens with nibs and all that sort of stuff. Ink monitors had to wash 'em out. They used to have these great big maps for geography lessons – we had to keep turning them over.

Percy Adams

Scary Tunnel

At the bottom of the school playground at the Church School there was a forbidden area. It was a disused air-raid shelter which was built partially underground. The only way in was a very low, cold and creepy tunnel. It was scary to crawl down there.

Angela Dursley

Stiff Collars

I went to the Church School until I was fourteen years old. In the early days we boys all had stiff collars that cut into your neck. The girls wore pinnies over their frocks. Some children who had toys were allowed to take them to school, things like a drum or a doll.

Bert Baxter

Home to Lunch

When my brother and I were at the Church School we walked home for lunch as we

Bill Baxter at the Church School, c. 1913.

didn't think they cooked the greens properly. Those who caught the bus were allowed out at 11.55 a.m. – we left at that time too until one of the girls told the teacher that we walked and didn't catch the bus. We had to leave at twelve and walk that bit faster.

Mick Horsley

Lunch Break

We used to have about half an hour in the playground at the middle of the day. We never had anything to eat, no lunch at all, sometimes an apple or an orange if you were lucky. We played hopscotch, football, hoops and tops. We used to go to work with the tops; when we lived in Bridge Street we started off from home spinning tops along the way.

Percy Adams

The Cane

There was no Catholic school in Witham so I went to Chelmsford by bus. We were taught by the Sisters of Mercy who were very strict; our hands were often swollen from the cane and I suppose we deserved it most of the time.

Pat Gillen

Miss Welland

I was born in a little bungalow used as a nursing home at the top of Collingwood Road. Nurse Hinds was in charge. I went to Chipping Hill Infants' before going to the Church School in Guithavon Street. I remember the headmistress, Miss Welland;

she was very strict and if we had done anything wrong we made sure we kept out of her way.

Ken Smith

Scholarship

I went to Chipping Hill Infants' in 1939 and then to the Church School in Guithavon Street before gaining a scholarship to Chelmsford High School. I remember sitting in the shelters during the war; they were situated just inside Chipping Hill School gate, next to the wall.

Daphne LeSage

Hot Pies

Mr Cranfield, the headmaster, lived in the house attached to the Church School. It had a large garden with apple trees. When the apples were ripe the masters placed a long line of them on the edge of the path near the school and lined the boys up on the path the other side of the road. At the given signal, 'hot pies', by the master, the boys raced across the road and grabbed as many as they could hold in their arms. This was not very good and totally unfair, as some boys were pushed over and small boys only got a few apples to take home.

Fred Gaymer

Slate Pencils

The teachers used to send you out to sharpen your slate pencil against the wall.

The Collingwood Road nursing home, today a private residence.

We used it to write on our slates. We loved it and tried to make a loud screaming noise as we scraped the pencils along the bricks.

Percy Adams

'Sniffer Sawdy'

Mr R.C. Sawdy was the headmaster and he was always called 'Sniffer Sawdy'. He was very loyal to the school and strongly supported the sports teams by turning up for matches held on Saturdays and after school. He congratulated them on their performance at morning assembly, regardless of whether they won or lost. Mr Cooper, a science teacher, I remember always wrote with green ink.

Mick Horsley

The Netball Team

I went to the Church School, where my teachers were Miss Welland, Miss Ambrose and Miss Gentry. I was in the netball team and we played matches against other local schools.

Eileen Smith

Barely Tall Enough

After school another adventure my friends and I would have was to play in St Nicholas' church on Chipping Hill. We would pretend to be the Vicar and give sermons from the pulpit, although we were barely tall enough to look over the edge. We would also pretend to be in the choir. Although we were very careful not to damage anything, part of the excitement was the fear of being caught.

Angela Dursley

Percussion Band

We taught the children music and movement. We used the radio because our equipment was limited. We also started a school band with percussion instruments. This was so successful that we had pupils from other schools wanting to join. All expenses were paid by the Essex County Council.

Grace Rose

Uncle Arthur

I remember a man we called Uncle Arthur. He used to walk up Church Street playing an accordion-type instrument. The children loved him and used to follow him to the Sunday school being held in the Bethel Chapel.

Pat Taylor

Nitty Nora

Nitty Nora came to the school once a month unless there was an epidemic. We hung our head over the desk and she inspected it by pushing the hairs apart. They used to put oil or something on your head if they found you had nits.

Albert Poulter

Eight-foot Wall

There was an eight-foot wall between the girls and the boys in the school playground. Any boy who was brave enough to climb and look over risked six of the best. The old head had eyes where no-one else had 'em!

Percy Adams

CHAPTER 3

Earning a Living

J.B. Slythe Monumental Masons today.

The Cattle Market

The Cattle Market used to be where the Labour Hall is today. We used to herd the cattle down the middle of the road to the slaughterhouse, which was near The Chase. The cattle arrived at the station from all over the place. It was a big goods yard and Witham was a proper junction then. Goods of all descriptions were shifted through there. I can remember picking up bricks and loading them onto lorries. We shifted over 36,000 one week – I worked until the blood ran out of my fingers. After the war, they started building morning, noon and night.

Reg Edwards

Ernie and the Piano

We had a flat-bed push cart and started work at about 6.30 a.m. I wore a big apron with two big pockets for the tools. Later in

Police Inspector Ron Shayshutt.

the morning I went back home for a breakfast of bread and butter; perhaps if we were lucky there might be some home-made jam. After that I probably met Ernie on the way to pick up a piano or some other piece of heavy furniture that people couldn't shift on their own.

Bert Baxter

Bus Driver

I was born in 1943 and we lived at 29 Church Street. My father John, known as Jack, was a bus driver for Moore's of Kelvedon which in 1962 was taken over by Eastern National. I had two brothers. I always wanted to join the Merchant Navy but my father would not allow it.

Ken Smith

Three Shillings a Day

The station gave you three clear days to empty a truck-load of coal; beyond that you paid demurrage of 3s a day. My father didn't approve of holidays and once when I'd had a fortnight off, which was quite a long holiday to take then, I came back and found a row of trucks to be unloaded. He said it was my fault the demurrage had built up.

Ken Thompson

Etching Another Name

My father, who lived to be over ninety, worked for Slythe the mason and often had to walk many miles to Wickham Bishops

Jack Smith, bus driver.

and surrounding areas. He would be sent to repair or clean the gravestones or to etch in another name. My father, who didn't have any form of transport, also had to carry his tools around with him; I think he may have had a trolley of sorts. My older sister often enjoyed walking with him.

Vera Howell

No Radios

There was no radio communication in the police force in 1965, so officers had fixed points and times, then waited for five minutes outside specified public phones. In Witham it was a five-strong shift and there were three shifts a day. Initially there were two sergeants and the CID consisted of a sergeant and a constable.

Ron Shayshutt

Telegraph Poles

As well as selling and delivering coal my father also carted telegraph poles and bricks. It would take them a whole day to cart them as far afield as Maldon.

Ken Thompson

Bridge and Park View

I worked for a few weeks at Bridge Hospital. I recall working in a trench when a young

Ken Smith's paternal grandfather at Park View.

A group photograph of Witham police with Inspector Shayshutt.

lad wearing a sheriff's badge appeared and shouted 'Stick 'em up!' It gave me quite a scare, of course, but it was just one of the residents having a bit of fun. After working on Bridge Hospital Assembly Hall, I then went to help with the finishing stages at Park View. My grandfather went to live there shortly afterwards. Before that, when I first started work at fifteen, I was a plumber's mate for Crittall's at Silver End. I earned £2 9s 2d per week. I used to give my mum £1 and had the rest for myself.

Ken Smith

Cooper Taber

I can recall when the railway had horses in a field at Easton Road. When I started work at Cooper Taber the seed was delivered to the warehouse from the railway. There was a turntable where the Maldon line branched off. The trucks were halted on the turntable; it was then turned round and the horses harnessed. Then they pulled the trucks up to the side of Cooper Taber to be unloaded.

Ken Thompson

£12 a Month

Generally speaking before the war a young constable earned £12 a month. I remember being at a Federation Conference in the sixties when a speaker said the day will come when a constable will receive £1,000 per annum. He was laughed out of the conference. Witham didn't have a section house but the constables received a rent allowance.

Ron Shayshutt

Braintree Road coal yard.

Carting it Loose

We bought the coal through a factor. It was delivered to the coal yards at the railway station. There were three siding tracks into the yards. We shovelled it into lorries if we were carting it loose and then bagged it on delivery to the customers, or we bagged it in the coal yard and people picked it up themselves.

Ken Thompson

Apprenticeship

I started at Marconi as an apprentice instrument maker. My first pay packet was for £1 19s gross. I didn't earn enough to pay tax, but my National Insurance contribution was 3s 6d. My monthly rail ticket was 19s 9d and I paid 10s a week for my keep. Out of what was left I had to buy my clothes and college books.

Mick Horsley

Bellamy's the Chemist

At fourteen I left the Church School and started work as an errand boy for Bellamy's the Chemist. There was no bike so I walked everywhere to make his deliveries and collections. We got the empty 10oz whisky bottles from Drake's the licensed retailer, then washed them out in a tank. When they were thoroughly cleaned, the chemist would fill them with medicines, usually cough stuff or bismuth and peppermint.

Bert Baxter

Rag and Bone Man

The rag and bone man came round frequently. We would buy a rabbit for a shilling or perhaps less than that, and we'd sell the skin to the rag and bone man for twopence or if lucky threepence. They also had a separate collection for garments made of wool – they gave a few pence for them, they never gave you much for it at all.

Fred Gaymer

Ernie Nichols

I remember Fleuty's Yard and Ernie Nichols, who was a wheelwright there. He used to make hand barrows and things. He had a big lathe – it was only a treadle really. They made naves – you know, they fitted over the centre of the wheels.

Fred Gaymer

Two Murders

I remember two bad periods, one when there were two murders and five attempted murders – all those cases were solved. The other was when there were eleven deaths on the Witham railway: some were suicide, some accidental.

Ron Shayshutt

Seabrooks at Boreham

My first job was for Seabrooks at Boreham. They had a nursery and were fruit growers. My take-home pay was £2 2s 4d and I

Ken Smith's maternal grandfather, Joe Jessie.

worked from 7 a.m. to 5 p.m. Mondays to Fridays and from 7 to 11 a.m. Saturday. I gave £1 to my mum, saved £1 and had 2s 4d pocket money.

John Ashcroft

Lionel Whiting

I worked with Lionel Whiting, a carpenter who was deaf and dumb. He was pleased with me because, being a carpenter like him, I knew what tools he needed and had them ready for him. He was a very good workman and the outside staircase we built at Coker and Rice is still being used.

Bert Baxter

Prisoners

Prisoners were held overnight in the cells at Witham. I remember one particular night when there were as many as seven. There were three cells, one kept for females, the other for males, though I can't ever remember a female being held overnight. Also there was a barred exercise courtyard where a PC would take out a prisoner for up to half an hour depending on his length of stay and how many other prisoners there were. My wife provided food for the prison inmates; one Sunday she did seven lunches.

Ron Shayshutt

The Ives Family

My mother always said that five generations of her family, the Ives, kept the forge at Chipping Hill. Mr Quoy's father took it off my great great great-grandfather on my mother's side. Later Mr Quoy's son continued working the forge.

Dennis Johnson

Paper Round

I did a paper round first for a little shop up Church Street; I earned 7s 6d. My father made me bank 6s and I had the remaining 1s 6d to spend. I then delivered groceries on an old tradesman's bike for the Braintree Road Co-op. I earned 12s 6d for that and if I worked Saturdays as well it was 18s.

Ken Smith

Old Jo Glover

Old Jo Glover gave me some advice I never took. He spoke to me one day when I just started work. 'Workin', then, boy?' 'Yeah!' 'What're you workin' for?' 'Money!' 'You've got it backwards.' 'What do you mean?' 'You get yer money and then make it work for you.' 'Where do I get the money from?' He never did tell me.

Percy Adams

Done the Job Properly

The laundry down Mill Lane employed about five or six women, who probably earned 29s 3d a week like most labourers those days. They used big coppers made of real copper – vats that were bricked in. Then they scrubbed hard with Sunlight or Lifebuoy soap. After rinsing the laundry out, it was hung on big lines in the yard. Women used to do the ironing – they done the job properly. It was collected and returned to customers by horse and cart.

Fred Gaymer

Adams and Mortimer

Bert Adams was a carpenter and Gerry Mortimer a painter, decorator and undertaker.

They joined forces to become Adams and Mortimer Builders.

Percy Adams

Direction of Labour

In 1948 they used to have what they called 'Direction of Labour'. You were sent on a job by the Labour Exchange and you had to take it, else there was no dole money. When I was stood off by Adams and Mortimer, where I

The forge at Chipping Hill.

45

Fred Gaymer's maternal grandfather, Ezekiel Thake.

used to earn 3s 3d an hour, I was sent to Ratcliffes at Durward Hall. They offered me the going rate of 2s 9d an hour as a carpenter. They told me only cabinet makers earned 3s 6d an hour.

Dennis Johnson

Benton Hall

There was an estate on the outskirts of Witham of which part is now the Benton Hall Golf Course. My grandfather, Ezekiel Thake, was very proud to be farm foreman over all of that.

Fred Gaymer

Not a Farthing Out

In the summer holidays I once worked for Mr Reg Leigh on the Co-op milk round. I collected the money on a Saturday and wrote out the chits. I paid the money and the chits into the Co-op Bank and, of course, they had to tally – any loss would be stopped from my wages of £2 0s 6d. Mr Leigh said, 'He's a good lad: not a farthing up nor a farthing down, not once.'

Mick Horsley

Town Beat

In 1965 two PCs split night duties and did four hours in the office and four hours on the town beat. When you lose a local PC walking his beat you lose the connection with the public. After twenty-five years walking the beat you were worn out: the average person only lasted eight years on his pension before dying.

Ron Shayshutt

Part-time Work

We all went pea-, bean- and fruit-picking in season. Mum worked part-time sorting seeds at the factory and cleaning at the White Hart public house. Clothing was scarce and Mum brought home children's clothes given to her by someone at the White Hart. They were too big so she had to put a tuck in everything. I remember one outfit which consisted of fur boots and a summer skirt.

Shirley Harper

Co-op Shares

I went to work in the Co-op in 1955. I was about fifteen and I worked as a clerk sorting the share slips into order. I earned about £2 a week at first.

Pat Taylor

A Real Giant

On the day I was to start work as a nanny I used the back door to the pub which led into the kitchens. I was very slim in those days and only 4ft 8ins tall, so when the door was opened by a six-foot kitchen maid I felt very small. In the kitchen I met the chef; he was at least 6ft 4ins – a real giant of a man. The waitress was also over 6ft and Mrs Hunt, my new boss, was tall. As I was taken to the nursery, I was hoping the children would be a normal height!

Ida Cunningham

Horse-drawn Cattle Float

My father had a horse-drawn cattle float. I remember carting the last pigs away from the farm. They were pregnant gilts and had to be looked after, you see.

Fred Gaymer

Night Soil Operators

My dad said there used to be winter water-closets and night soil operators who collected the full buckets through a flap as

Witham railway station today.

47

big as a doormat on the outside wall. They did the rounds nightly, emptying the buckets into containers on a horse and cart before returning the buckets through the hatch.

Fred Willshire

Crittall's Factories

Old man Crittall, Valentine's father, made one window frame in his blacksmith's shop in Braintree, sold that and that was the start of Crittall factories.

Percy Adams

Mr McQuinn

When I served behind the counter at the chemist's, Mr McQuinn, a Scotsman who lived on the premises, told me to persuade people to buy the big bottles. The prices were 1s 3d and 2s 6d. I was paid 10s a week; they were nice people to work for. I left after eighteen months, though they wanted me to take it up and train to be a chemist.

Bert Baxter

The Union

If you belonged to the Union it was dodgy to get a job, especially with small firms. These employers knew who was a good chap and who wasn't and they also knew who belonged to a Union and who didn't.

Dennis Johnson

Plaster of Paris

I knew Captain Abrey's son Tom well. Because of an affliction he had a plaster of Paris cast on his body the whole of his life. When I was a window cleaner I can remember seeing in his bedroom that he had erected ropes and swivels to enable him to get out of bed unaided.

Albert Poulter

90,000 Boxes

At the fruit-packing factory my wife earned £2 3s a week as a grader and packer of apples. I earned £4 15s a week. It was very busy some weeks and we had as many as 90,000 boxes – and each apple was hand-wrapped in tissue paper. The fruit came in from all the fruit growers around. We worked a 44-hour week.

Pat Smith

Co-op Drapery

I went as a nursing maid to a local family, but after that I went as an apprentice to the Co-op drapery department. It was three years' training at about 5s a week. They taught us all the drapery trade which they don't bother to do today. In those days you had to block them and roll them as the material arrived in layers. I think we sold it for about 1s 6d a yard. After they opened a little shop in Hatfield Peverel they asked me to run it. I got paid about 15s a week for that.

Vera Howell

Charlie Warren

Next to the Swan, where Ginetta's was, Charlie Warren had the West End Garage. There were four pumps – Shell, National Benzole, Pratts and Dominion. Prices were from 1s 1d to 1s 4d. Charlie Warren had a van and he went back and forth between Hatfield Peverel and Rivenhall. It was painted blue one side and red the other, so most people thought he had two vans. Charlie went in the RAF and never came back from the war.

Percy Adams

Mrs Crittall's Wedding Gift

My wife went to The Manor where the Crittall's lived when it first opened. It was really a weekend house for them. Mrs Crittall was ever so nice: she allowed the boyfriends to come in for a very good evening meal and popped into the kitchen to ask if we enjoyed it. My wife used to help as parlour maid when they had parties. Mrs Crittall gave her silk for her wedding dress and paid for a proper dressmaker to make it.

Fred Gaymer

In the Sewing Room

I worked in the sewing room as a seamstress making nurses' uniforms. I used a treadle machine. The uniforms were made out of heavy cotton. We didn't make the starched hats – they were made elsewhere.

Rose Willshire

Late Deliveries

I used to work for the International as a delivery boy when I was young. The last delivery on a Saturday was really late. I cycled down Cut Throat Lane to a farm cottage – there were no places, no buildings, no lights, no nothing, just meadows there. I didn't finish till about nine o'clock most Saturdays.

Reg Edwards

Spread Eagle

I got an increase from 8s a week to 15s; that's why I came to Witham in 1941. I worked for the Hunts; they had two children and they were the landlords at the Spread Eagle. Mr Hunt had been conscripted into the Army as a major.

Ida Cunningham

Prescription Delivery

Bill Adams was a postman. When he did outlying areas he picked up their prescriptions and delivered the medicine the next day.

Albert Poulter

Magistrates

When I was in charge we had an excellent relationship with Witham District Council – Mr Crook the clerk, Mr Sparrow and Mr Belair the engineers. Also a most excellent understanding with the local Bench. I told

Rose Willshire as lollipop lady.

all my constables that you must never try to deceive magistrates or you lose their trust.

Ron Shayshutt

Credit Draper

I worked as a draper's assistant for Heddles – he was a bespoke and credit draper. People could pay for their goods weekly at one shilling in the pound spent. He employed three or four salesmen who travelled the villages with sample and pattern books. Two buyers carried the materials, shoes, etc. backwards and forwards on the train from warehouses in London.

Dennis Johnson

Lollipop Lady

In 1965 I was the first lollipop lady in Witham, standing between Spinks Lane and Howbridge Road every morning and afternoon. The uniform was provided and I earned 19s 6d a week.

Rose Willshire

Fourth Housemaid

My wife lived up Church Street. She went to work as a nursemaid to the painters and decorators Lille's of Colchester; they opened a shop opposite the Spread Eagle. Then she went to work at Terling Place as a fourth housemaid.

Fred Gaymer

Cullen's Trials

My mother worked for Cullen's on the trial grounds in the summer and in the warehouse in the winter. They were wholesalers and sold seeds in bulk. Each time a batch was sold, Cullen's had to have trials.

John Ashcroft

Generous Tips

I worked at the Spread Eagle as a waitress. I worked long hours and earned £2 per week plus generous tips. Mr Evans was the manager at the time. We used to have regular people and a good set meal cost 6s.

Mary Gillen

Hoisting the Coal

My father was a very strong man. He lifted the coal bags onto his back with one arm. He was unable to use the other arm to hoist the coal because of the bullet wound he received in the war.

Ken Thompson

Chimney Sweeps

My dad, Dick Willshire, was a stoker at Bridge Hospital and also one of the local chimney sweeps. Dad had a push bike and Dodman, another sweep who lived next to Bethel Chapel, had a horse and cart. They had a good relationship as there was plenty of work. Everyone had coal fires then. He charged about 2s 6d to sweep the chimney and clean up. Some people wanted the soot for their gardens; otherwise he bagged it and carted it away on his bike.

Fred Willshire

The Huntsmen

My mother and aunt used to do a bit of catering. I remember a special floor being put down in the Public Hall for the huntsmen. They had a meal set out on trestles on the stage and they rode their horses right into the hall. My aunt Mrs

Heddell's the bespoke tailors used as offices today.

Chaplin arranged the meal. You wouldn't believe it these days, would you?

Vera Howell

Coker and Rice

I was about sixteen when I started work for Coker and Rice, the upholsterer in 69 High Street. We went to all the big houses. At The Grove I mainly saw the butler, the head housemaid or the footman, but I didn't see anything of Mr Lawrence. We took the carpets outside and beat them until all the dust was gone. It could take hours, especially the red Turkish one from the dining room. They could hear if I stopped beating and would come out to see why.

Bert Baxter

Coal Rations

After I did my National Service in 1954 I started work for my father. At that time a hundredweight of coal cost 6s 7d and was rationed to 34cwt a year. We didn't always get paid on time and had to collect the last week's payment before delivering the next load.

Ken Thompson

Nurses' Home

I started work at Ivy Chimneys in 1953. It was a nurses' home then and I was a trainee assistant cook. There were about fourteen nurses living there and I earned £4 19s 6d for a 48-hour week.

Fred Willshire

Richardson & Wakelin.

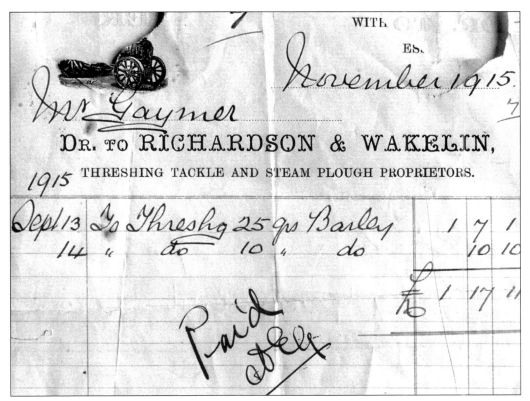

A bill from Richardson & Wakelin dated 1915.

Two Tumbrils

We had two: I had a tumbril and Dad had a tumbril. We used them when we shifted sand and gravel and that sort of thing.

Fred Gaymer

Bottle of Stout

I was an office boy to Bright who was then Clerk to the Council. He paid me 4s a week 'cos my mother was a widow. All cheques had to be signed by a councillor, so I would be sent to Captain Abrey. After he signed the cheque he would reach into his pocket and say in his gruff voice, 'There you are, boy – tell your mother to buy a bottle of stout.'

Albert Poulter

Richardson and Wakelin

There used to be a blacksmith's shop here years ago, 'cos this yard was hired out from the Honourable Strutts to Richardson and Wakelin. They had six or seven thresh and tackle complete with barn work, elevators and chaff cutters. Then they had two pairs of steam plough engines.

Fred Gaymer

Big Houses

When I worked for Coker and Rice I went to Lord Rayleigh's, Du Cane's at Totham, all the big houses, and Roslyn House where Miss Bevington, a spinster, was really mistress of the house then. I was earning 10s to 12s a week there, then Coker died or something and left Mr Rice to run it.

Bert Baxter

Saturday Round

When I was fifteen I worked on the Co-op milk round on Saturdays. I earned six bob a day. For that money, I had to deliver to Guithavon Road, Blunts Hall, Cuppers Close, Highfield Road, the Victoria pub, Powers Hall, Chipping Hill and Church Street. I had to go back to the dairy to unload the empties and pick up more milk. It was a pretty modern dairy, but always wet under foot. In the winter it was very cold. I wore an old raincoat which had grease all down the side from the milk crates. The Union chap pushed for more money for me and the rate was upped to 10s a day.

Mick Horsley

Old Fire Engine

The original fire engine was an old lorry with a 500-gallon tank strapped on the back. A pump with another pump behind and a ladder on the top, and that was it!

Percy Adam

Percy Adams and a crew of firefighters.

CHAPTER 4

At Leisure

Post-war bathing suits.

Public Hall Dance

One evening there was a dance at the Public Hall and as we were doing the refreshments for the band we were allowed in free. I got someone to mind the children I used to look after and got dressed, then I went to meet the rest of the staff in the Tap Bar which was across the yard. It was dark and I ran out of the back door as I was late, and smashed into a car. It was parked too close to the door. I bashed my nose and when I reached the Tap Bar my face looked a real mess. My friends helped me disguise the bruises, but whenever I stepped into the dance hall they played *Two Lovely Black Eyes!*

Ida Cunningham

Fluety's Yard

Fluety was a wheelwright, where the RAF Club is now. When we were kids we used to go round there, especially when he had got a fire up. We used to sit round the fire and watch as they heated the iron bands up to put on the wheels.

Percy Adams

Dick Meads

When I worked for my father before I married, I can remember one hot day when I was hoeing the field for Everett the milkman, behind Spring Lodge. I stopped the horse, and while he had a bit of grass I went to 'Dick Meads' bathing place. I had my lunch of cheese and ham and a drink of cold tea in a bottle.

Fred Gaymer

I Played Full-back

As a young man I played full-back for Witham football team. They played in the Essex and Suffolk Border League and were quite good. We had a lot more support than there is now.

Ken Thompson

Constance Close

Nicky Nocks was made famous round here in the First World War. Soldiers from the Engineering Corps were billeted everywhere and they used to court the local girls, taking them down to the river near Constance Close. There were lovely trees there, especially horse chestnuts, along that walk.

Albert Poulter

Witham Swimming Club

There used to be a Witham Swimming Club at the 'Pea Hole'. There was a temporary building provided, to be used for clothes changing. Well, after several years this portable building was plastered with different notes and drawings – you'd have a job to find a spot on the board that was clear. When the club packed up my father bought the shed off them and we rebuilt it in the yard here as Dad's office. Well, of course, we had to cover all the markings on it, didn't we. We daren't let my mother see them!

Fred Gaymer

Courting Room

Mrs De'ath and Ruby the barmaid at the Woolpack were full of life and curious about everything. They used to have this funny little room for courting couples. It was near the door and you had to be given permission to use it.

Ken Smith

Raffia and the Wireless

We had a wireless with wet-cell batteries that cost you fourpence to recharge – it wasn't very much. The children would sit round the table doing raffia work or knitting while they listened. Perhaps there'd be a play on, and you could hear a pin drop while they worked away with their hands and listened to the play.

Connie Edwards

Marina Lake

I always had a cycle. My father bought my first one for me; it was second hand and cost thirty bob from Mr Glover's. As lads, in the six weeks' school holiday we would cycle to Maldon for a dip in the Marina Lake, so called as Princess Marina had opened it.

John Hollick

Church House

Church House in Church Street was our favourite place to play 'Knock Down Ginger'. It was brilliant, as the door was near the edge of the path and we could take off easily.

Angela Dursley

Races at Newmarket

The factors arranged outings for coal merchants, as a kind of thank-you for doing business with them. My father and I went on trips to the races at Newmarket. We also went to Nottingham, where we went down to the pit face. It was always a good day out.

Ken Thompson

A Lovely Courting Place

The Grove Avenue was such a lovely courting place. It was a private road but we were allowed to walk through. They were all lime trees. It was decided to cut all the trees and build on it; my father bought all the trees after they were felled. A lot of it went

Ken Thompson on a coal trade outing.

Lime trees in The Avenue.

as firewood, of course – we towed a portable saw bench there and took it out load by load. We never paid much for them; they were just glad for somebody to clear them. Lime is what they use for carving: a very close-grain wood, fairly soft, a certain firmness about it. Grinling Gibbons, who did marvellous carving in London, was able to carve a five-inch ivy leaf as thin as a real ivy leaf – that was all done with lime.

Fred Gaymer

Boat Races

In our spare time on a Wednesday afternoon we played football or cycled to Heybridge.

We took out a rowing boat for a shilling off Mrs Easter who lived next door to a pub called The Wave, and we rowed to Beeleigh Falls, which was as far as you could go. There were two boats and with two in each boat we used to race each other.

Dennis Johnson

Air Guns

We had some advantages: we had the meadow and Dad didn't mind me having the boys in to play football and a little cricket, and of course we used our air guns for target practice.

Fred Gaymer

Cricket

We used to play cricket where All Saints' is. When the ecclesiastical people bought the land for a church and a school we moved to Maldon Road. We all wore whites, some of them second hand. August Bank Holiday week was a cricket week: on the Monday we played the Essex Hunt – they used to come through on their horses and with their dogs. The Master of the Hunt lived at Lawn House. We used to play through the week – Frinton, Clacton – and at the end we played at the Essex Club and ground. The people from Essex Cricket Club always annoyed me. Stan Nicholls, who I'd say was one of the best cricketers in the country for years, he used to take a hundred wickets and score a thousand runs for Essex, and he used to come and play us at Witham.

Percy Adams

Places to Play

As youngsters, we had many places to play, including the allotments and recreation ground. We would walk alongside the cemetery to join Rectory Lane, Motts Lane and Cut Throat Lane to the railway line and on to Rivenhall End, by the school. There is still a bit of Rectory Lane left, but the rest is all joined up. There was Half Hyde Farm, Lewis's and Mr Wells' land where he kept horses and had a market garden.

Mick Horsley

Pelan Polish

At the Co-op Treat there was a shoe-polishing competition. If you won, you got a tin of Pelan Polish from Scotland and a polishing cloth.

Jean Johnson

Church Youth Club

I used to go to the Church Youth Club which met in the Church House. It is now used by the Army cadets and is opposite the Labour Hall.

Daphne LeSage

Rose and George

Children came to Witham from Poplar in London during the summer for a holiday in

Church House today, almost unchanged.

Coronation cake.

the country. Mrs Harris from Church Street took in half a dozen and she had a tent in the garden which was used as a mess hall. There were two or three batches, each one staying for a couple of weeks. We played with them and it seemed to me that the girls were all called Rose and the boys George.

Dennis Johnson

Bridge Home

Most Sunday mornings the boys from Bridge Home marched to All Saints', led by their brass band. They all looked very smart in their red uniforms and with shining brass instruments. They always sat in the back rows of the church. We often watched them re-form outside after the service and start their march back.

Fred Gaymer

Coronation

We had a terrific party for the Coronation in 1953. There were about 120 children. We decided to make them fancy dress – I ended up making about six fancy dresses. My oldest, Colin, was a clown and little Kelvin was a Dutch boy. The street winner got a little watering can from Lady Strutt. The following day there was a party for the 'lah-di-dahs' at the Public Hall. They hadn't got enough children so they came up and begged us to take our children. Colin didn't want to go as a clown so he went as a golliwog. The 'lah-di-dahs', of course, had hired their costumes, but old Sister Hinds said, 'The golliwog takes first prize.' He got a bar of chocolate.

Ida Cunningham

Cover Your Bets

I remember the year Airborne won the Grand National. It was a long shot at 60 to 1. Every member of a certain family backed it. My father took a chance; it was a rank outsider and he decided not to cover his bets. Airborne won and I don't think my father spoke for a week.

Jean Johnson

Rock 'n' Roll

I liked rock 'n' roll, Bill Haley especially. I listened to the juke box: it cost 2s 6d for three tunes. I also had an old-fashioned tape recorder, but I also liked sport and I watched Witham Town Football Club. Some of the lads from school played for them. Tim Keeble was goalie. I sometimes went to watch Ipswich and Chelmsford as well. My friends and I used to go to hear Sonny Butler play the piano and sing in the White Hart Tap. It was crowded, as everyone went there on a Saturday night to hear Sonny.

Ken Smith

Horticultural Society

I was on the committee of the Horticultural Society for years. They used to hire the tents on Witham recreation ground. That was costly and they used to buy a 'noner' of beer for the men who did the work. The tents always got damaged a bit so you wanted a nightwatchman there really. They used to hire the Public Hall all day just for the evening dance, so I voted to hold the show in the Public Hall instead of at the recreation ground.

Fred Gaymer

Thirsty Heifers

I went with my dad, uncle and cousin to Blue Mills, fishing. On one occasion my cousin and I were mucking about and being very noisy and we were sent off in case we scared the fish away. We stood on a bridge and watched as a lorry drew up. We saw the driver get out and open the back to let out a herd of heifers. They were so thirsty they ran straight to the river. My shocked father and uncle jumped into the river to escape; we just stood on the bridge, laughing!

Shirley Harper

The Pea Hole

The Council went down the back of the rubbish dump and they dug out a swimming place in the river just after the Blackwater joins the Brain. We called it the 'Pea Hole'. The Council even put up a hut for us to change in, an open-fronted hut. Of course, we never had any costumes – we didn't have any money. The girls used to wear their drawers sometimes.

Percy Adams

A postcard from Southend.

Seaside

When I was about four, my parents would take my sister and me by steam train to Southend. We would spend our holiday with my aunt and uncle and my boy cousin. My uncle had a butcher's shop in the town where we stayed. I remember these as very happy holidays at the seaside.

Vera Howell

Trundling Hoops

During dry weather, boys and girls bowled hoops along the road to and from school. The girls used wooden hoops and a short stick to trundle their hoops. The boys used blacksmith-made iron hoops and iron sliders as we called them, also made by the blacksmith. A piece of round iron with a handle one end and a hook the other end. The faster you could run, the better the hoop trundled.

Fred Gaymer

Rifle Cups

My father and I won a few cups for rifle shooting from the Braintree and District Rifle League, which I think is still going.

Fred Gaymer

Dropped Catch

When I was about seventeen years old I started playing cricket and football for Witham. We played matches in all the surrounding towns and villages. In my career as a cricketer I went in from no. 1 to no. 11 in the batting order and I also bowled quite a bit. I remember making a mess of one catch and breaking my finger; needless to say, I dropped the ball. My wife Ann also liked sport and played tennis, hockey and squash locally.

John Hollick

Day Trips to Maldon

As a child I would be taken to Maldon. The prams and pushchairs would go in the guard's van. We would get very excited as we passed Langford and we knew we were nearly there. We took our food with us but I thought it was really posh when my dad would buy a tray with a pot of tea for 2s 6d.

Pat Gillen

Pictures Mayhem

Saturday mornings I would go with my two elder sisters to the pictures at the Whitehall. As well as feature films they ran serials that we followed. When the children caused mayhem the man in charge would go on the stage after putting the lights on and stopping the film. He would give everyone a stern warning before restarting the film.

Angela Dursley

Susan Hayward

In the 1950s I remember living at the Red Lion for a short while when my parents looked after the pub for Mr and Mrs Terry. They went on holiday to America to visit Mrs Terry's family. She was related to Eileen Terry, the famous actress. I visited the Whitehall cinema opposite to see Susan Hayward in a film where she was due to go to the electric chair. The film broke down and the audience had to leave without ever seeing the end. I believe it was a common occurrence.

Diane Watson

Memorable Mr Swift

My mother occasionally went to Bethel church, so I went to the Sunday school there. The teachers were Mr Swift, two Mr Dawsons, a Mr Heard and a Mr Redley. Mr Swift was quite memorable: he seemed to me a very powerful speaker and got his message over. I always took notice of what he said.

Ken Smith

Witham Cricket Club

Witham Cricket Club shared their ground with Crittall's Cricket Club. Crittall's paid the groundsman and Witham contributed. My father, Tom Ashcroft, was secretary of the WCC. He played for them before the war and was a founder member of the restart in 1946. The last game he played there was in 1956. He helped many under-eighteen players, including Bill Coleman, John and Tom Cullen, Charles Tabor, Barry Wakelin and Freddie Goodchild. The manager of the White Hart, Mr Pamplin, played too. Later, Alan Byford, Derek Bright and Mr King the jeweller were also in the team.

John Ashcroft

Witham Football Ground

The Witham football team used to play on the pitch to the rear of the Grove House. It was quite a way back and the lane leading to it started where the back of Stoffer's chemist is situated. The Grove pitch was one of the best football grounds in the county and lots of visiting teams came for matches there. I think Mr Lawrence owned The Grove at that time.

Fred Gaymer

Sound Effects

The cinema shows on a Saturday morning at the Public Hall cost twopence. Joy Clark was manager and it was bedlam! If it was a war film someone would bang on a tin bath for sound effects. The pianist played according to what was on the screen.

Dennis Johnson

The Rubbish Tip

We used to go onto the rubbish tip. When they emptied the rubbish there was what seemed like thousands of kids sorting through it. Well, actually, I got my first bike off it – a wheel here and a wheel there and a pedal somewhere else – and I built it up and made a bike out of it.

Percy Adams

Follow the River

In those days we kids would have our breakfast and then meander and play all day; if we didn't go home for hours, nobody was worried. We would walk for miles in the fields and woods around Witham. One favourite walk was from beside the police station, across the meadow to Little Braxted, then follow the river all the way to Blue Mills.

Shirley Harper

Four Brothers in the Band

My three brothers and I played in the British Legion Band. We met for practice on a Monday night at the Band Hut, which was a small room at the rear of what is now the Mill Lane Stores. Ernie played the cornet, Ralph the bass and Richard the E-flat horn; I played the trombone. Mr Albert Knight, an ex-

Fred and Ernie Willshire.

Marine bandmaster, was in charge. The Legion provided uniforms and instruments if necessary. When we played at fêtes and carnivals the band had their expenses covered; of course, there was no expenses involved when we paraded on Remembrance Sunday.

Fred Willshire

Hockey Club

You know Collingwood Road, there were no houses on one side and at the top was a YMCA hut and it had tennis courts in the grounds. When I was about sixteen we formed a hockey team up there. Our dresses were white, quite long and made from 'Tustle silk'; we also wore white stockings.

Vera Howell

British Legion Rifle Club

The British Legion formed a rifle club after the war and my father and I joined that; then we formed Witham Rifle Club again. There was a 25-yard range and gun storage for the TA in Mill Lane.

Fred Gaymer

Cyril Ashby

I belonged to St Nicholas' church choir. At one point there were sixty-five members. The choirmaster was Cyril Ashby, who was an excellent organist. Henry Dorking the blacksmith sang baritone solos.

John Ashcroft

Fred Willshire with his trombone.

Films

At the cinema I saw Cliff Richard in *Summer Holiday* and Elvis in *Jailhouse Rock*.

Ken Smith

ack Butcher's Taxi

We went to dances at Wickham Bishops village hall. Five or six of us would hire Jack Butcher's taxi – it cost us about 2s each. Sometimes we had to walk. I remember a group called Leslie and the Downbeaters.

Pat Gillen

Snuff

It was more higher-class people who took snuff. Some of them kept it in antique silver boxes. We ordinary people smoked and drank when we could afford it.

Percy Adams

Snooker

In the room next to our bedroom at the police station there was a full-sized snooker table. At first it was terrible with the constant clicking of snooker balls as we tried to sleep, so Ron told the constables they had to finish by 10 p.m.

Sylma Shayshutt

Collar and Tie

The Crown was a 'spit and sawdust' place. The poshest pub was the Red Lion. They wouldn't serve you unless you had a collar and tie on.

Pat Smith

First Carnival

In 1951 to celebrate the Festival of Britain the local council asked the RAFA to organize a carnival. It was so successful that the RAFA carried on organizing it for twenty-six years until it was handed over to a local committee. In 1951 my brother-in-law had inherited the corner plot, where the RAFA clubhouse is, from his father. He then sold it to the RAFA for £310 in 1955.

Prior to that the RAFA had been established in Witham since 1944. Some of my fellow members included Wally Westgate, Maurice Colby, Ron Rogers, John Goldsmith and Richard Joslin.

Dennis Johnson

Blyth's Mill

I was never a fisherman but I think I remember seeing fishermen near Blyth's Mill. The river was right beside the road – that was the hold-up for the water wheel, you see.

Fred Gaymer

Roach and Small Pike

We went fishing where the Brain met the Blackwater at a place we used to call the 'Pea Hole'. We caught roach and small pike using home-made rods. They were made with bamboo canes and bent pins and we dug worms or used bread as bait. You only had thread as your fishing line, whereas now they use catgut or whatever. We also made our own reels from empty thread spools.

Fred Willshire

Dragon versus Morning Star

Quite a lot of people went to the pubs. In Bridge Street it was quite a sight when the Dragon and the Morning Star turned out.

Dennis Johnson (far left) and members of the RAFA Club.

They would fight each other until along came the police, hiked 'em on their backs and shoulders and then chucked 'em over the hedge into the field opposite the bridge.

Percy Adams

Chub That Got Away

I fished in the river at what we used to call the 'Diving Board', which was an old trunk that fell across the river down by the Chase as you go down into Moat Farm. We used to catch mostly sticklebacks, minnows and if you were lucky you might get a dace or two. I once hooked a nice chub, but unfortunately I never saw it – it was the one that got away.

Ken Smith

The Sign of the Werewolf

I remember going to the cinema when it cost a shilling to get in and you needed an adult to get into an 'A' film. We would hang around outside asking adults we knew to take us in. One time we went in and it frightened the life out of me: it was *The Sign of the Werewolf*.

Shirley Harper

The Misses Patterson

Every Easter the Misses Patterson used to hide Easter eggs in all the plants and bushes in their garden. Then they opened the gates and children were allowed to go in, find the eggs and keep them. They lived at

Pelican House which is now a children's nursery.

Albert Poulter

A Rifle Range

Just up Mill Lane on the right was a long shed which was used by Witham Rifle Club. My father did a lot of work there and brought the range up to a safe standard. Mr Groves the tailor was the prime mover of the rifle range at that time. They used .22 rifles and would buy the ammunition from the gunsmith Leeches of Chelmsford or from Mondy's who sold ammunition as well in those days.

Fred Gaymer

Colin Smith fishing locally.

Irish Dances

There were regular Irish dances at the British Legion Hut. It cost 2s 6d to get in. Two Englishmen from London came and played Irish music – they were brilliant. Father Burn put them up for the night. I met my wife Mary at a St Patrick's Day dance in Takeley forty-one years ago.

Pat Gillen

Jack Hubbard

It was wonderful: there were no cars so we could play in the road. I was a tomboy and was leader of a football team. There was one boy, Jack Hubbard, who didn't want me to play. His mother complained when we had a fight.

Hilda Pluck

Early Films

On Saturday afternoon the kids crammed into the Public Hall to see films before Witham had its own cinema.

Percy Adams

Frank's Café

There were caffs in Witham. Frank's Café was where the glass shop is now and there was one further up the High Street. We used to listen to the juke box and drink coffee or milkshakes – it was about 6d a drink. The cinema, which was run by the Gayes family who lived at Blue Mills, also

Witham cricket team.

had a café; it was run by Bob Fuller who used to be a bus driver.

Ken Smith

Pogo Stick

Mrs Coleman was previously Miss Brown, and her and I were christened on the same day in the parish church. She was something to do with the Wakelins. She always used to say how my father, who was estate carpenter, made her a pogo stick.

Fred Gaymer

Penny Machine

After the war you wouldn't get women in the pubs; that's what they used the Jug and Bottle for. Beer was 7d or 9d a pint. The George had skittles, shove ha'penny, and a penny machine. If you were successful on that you won a cigarette.

Pat Smith

Cricket Team

Ken, my husband, played cricket for the Witham team. I helped provide the teas. I seem to remember it was mainly cress, salad and sandwich spread. Also I had to take my turn in washing the whites. Ken remembers the team members were Paul Hollingsworth, John Hollick, Bill Denny, John Green, Roy Moss, Geoff Lang, Pete Champ, Ken Owers, Chris Pledger and Colin Elligott.

Maggie Thompson

St Nicholas' Church Choir

The church choir practised Tuesdays, boys only, and Fridays, full choir. When we sang *The Crucifixion* at Terling we needed a double-decker bus to take us all.

John Ashcroft

Cigarette Cards

Grandfather collected cigarette cards in albums. Mostly flowers, wildlife and nature, though he might have had a few football ones. I collected stamps for a short while.

Ken Smith

Band of Hope

I belonged to the Band of Hope. They used to announce the meetings at school. It cost a halfpenny a week and there were a dozen or so boys and girls that attended. I took the Pledge there as I thought what they said was good and I do not like either the smell or the taste of beer to this day.

Albert Poulter

The Cockies

The Cockies is still there today, between Bridge Street and Maldon Road. We went after we left school – took towels and paddled and swam.

Fred Gaymer

A recent view of Pelican House.

CHAPTER 5

Passing Trade

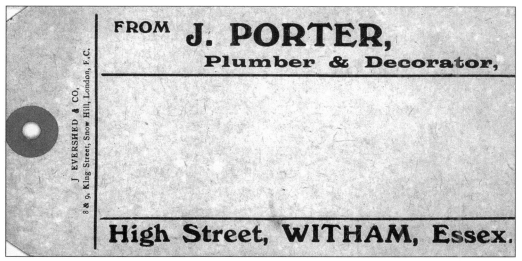

A label advertising J. Porter, plumber and decorator.

Mr Cutts the Fishmonger

On VE Day Mr Cutts the fishmonger was happily clapping and enjoying the big bonfire which had been lit in the High Street. He didn't find out until later that his privy was a major part of the bonfire!

Pat Gillen

Staple Diet

A big loaf of bread cost about twopence-halfpenny and a pint of milk about twopence. Before the war, Mr Newman used to bring the milk in a big churn on his horse and cart. Nothing so common as going to fetch it with your jug – he knocked on the door and brought it to you.

Connie Edwards

Next to Brand's the Bakers

After the war my father Jack used his £100 demob gratuity to start a shoe business. He hired a little shop between Mr Brand the baker and Cutts' fish shop, in the High

Old banger.

Street where the Woolwich is now. Then in 1950 my father bought the piece of waste ground in Maldon Road, next door to Houson and Clark the hairdressers. He hired local builders Adams and Mortimer to build his new shop.

John Hollick

Mr Porter the Plumber

I remember Mr Porter the plumber and decorator. He has a squint and one day when he was carrying a load he bumped into someone and said, 'Look where you're going.' He promptly got the reply, 'Why don't you go where you're looking?'

Fred Gaymer

Lynfield Motors

In 1962 I bought my first car, a Ford Esquire. It was a second-hand grey old banger which cost £200 from Lynfield Motors. They only sold second-hand cars then, they didn't have their dealership. When I started working for myself I bought a new car; it is the only one I've had. It was a Ford Anglia van from Deals of Kelvedon for £416. My first 500-mile service cost £2 1s 6d.

John Ashcroft

Mr Barren of Chipping Hill

With my Saturday morning fourpence I went to Mr Barren, a pork butcher at Chipping Hill. He also sold sweets and I

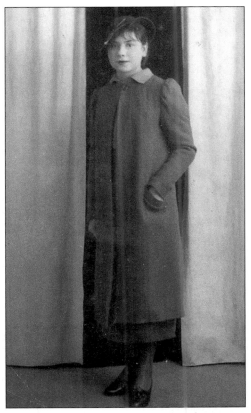

Miss Beatrice Lane.

bought a bar of Palm toffee. Sometimes I asked him for a round coconut square, which cost less than the toffee.

Dennis Johnson

The Corona Man

The Corona man would deliver to the door; he came every week. The bottles cost sixpence each and he collected the empties the following week.

Mary Gillen

Half Cow Size

The leather which was used to repair shoes and boots we bought in bales, big sheets, half cow size. Now we have to buy soles already cut out.

John Hollick

Sweethearts

My mother came to Witham with her family in 1936; they came from London. My grandfather owned several grocery shops and he opened another one in the High Street, where the *Braintree and Witham Times* used to be and Bawtree & Sons are now. They stayed for eighteen months before moving on to the coast. My mother was eighteen and she and her sister had met two local boys, so when the family moved away, they stayed in Witham and married their sweethearts.

Diane Watson

Open Doors

No-one locked their doors. The Heddle's collector would come to our house weekly to collect his money. Mum paid so much off their bill every week. When she was out working, my mother, like everybody else, would leave this money on the kitchen table. It was about lunchtime when he got to our house and Mum would let him make a cup of tea and eat his sandwiches in the kitchen.

Shirley Harper

Hollick's shoe shop.

Hollick's Shoe Shop

In 1950 my father Jack bought a piece of waste ground in Maldon Road next door to Houson and Clark, the hairdressers. He hired local builders Adams and Mortimer to build this shop.

John Hollick

Dibben's

The first time I went to the hairdresser's I went to Dibben's in the High Street and had my hair cut in a fashionable bob. My father, who thought young girls should wear their hair long, wasn't very pleased about it.

Vera Howell

Mr Brown the Baker

I was called up for National Service in 1954 and served with the Army Catering Corps. On discharge I went to work for Mr Brown, who had a bakery shop where the Health Store is now. He regaled us with tales of his experiences in the First World War.

Pat Gillen

Witham Bargain Centre

My father opened the Witham Bargain Centre in the High Street, where the *Braintree and Witham Times* were and opposite Balch & Balch. As the name suggests, he undercut other stores and also displayed his fruit outside on the pavement.

Jim Lane and his niece, Diane Watson, where the family business was in 1936.

Owing to fierce opposition from local traders he decided to close down and move on.

Jim Lane

Paper Cone of Sweets

We bought a pennyworth of broken chocolate from Mr Ellis's. For sixpence you could get a paper cone of liquorice pipes, gobstoppers, sherbet dabs with a toffee. I remember once trying an old dodge: I covered a farthing with silver paper, but all Mr Ellis said was, 'Well, Hilda, you're well off today.' He let me get away with it that time.

Hilda Pluck

Hocks of Bacon

Mr Hannah who had the stores in Braintree Road sold hocks of bacon for threepence each. It was extra revenue for him as he'd already made his money on the meat.

Mick Horsley

Bullock for Christmas

The cattle market day was on Tuesday. Mr Page walked across the top of the pens on double planks while he took the bidding. At Christmas a huge bullock was auctioned. Mr Greatrix, who had a butcher's shop, and others like Loveday and Sorrell's bid for it.

Dennis Johnson

General Store

I was fifteen when we sold the house in Wembley and my dad bought the general store in Church Street. He used to be an estate agent but soon learned the trade of a local grocer. He would get a whole side of bacon and many a time I stood and watched him doing all the different cuts.

Margaret Brannan

Houson & Clark

When we went to Houson & Clark the hairdresser in Maldon Road we would sit with our heads bowed and hope Mr Clark wouldn't accidentally cut us. He was deaf and would be unable to hear us if we

The General Store in Church Street.

76

The Willshire brothers at Carnival Day, 1957.

shouted 'ouch'. Mr Houson had already passed on. I would always have a short back and sides and it cost between 6d and 9d.

John Hollick

Lansdowne Restaurant

I remember people eating in Lansdowne Restaurant where the National Westminster is now. It started off as Day's Café with Roy Ingham as proprietor.

Fred Willshire

Dorothy Bidwell's

I used to buy clothes from the little shop opposite the Spread Eagle called Dorothy Bidwell's. A good quality dress was £5; I would take it across the road to the Spread Eagle where I lived and worked to try it on.

Mary Gillen

Swarm of Bees

Mr Dibben the hairdresser was well known for his love of bees. Someone would run into his shop and say, 'There's a swarm around,' and he would just leave his customer, sometimes half-shaved, while he dashed off to fetch the bees.

Albert Poulter

Too Tired for a Social Life

I was fifteen when I worked at my father's shop, and I earned 8s a week. The hours were long and I was too tired for any social life. We lived in the flat above the shop and the stairs from the shop were the only entrance to the flat. There were two bedrooms with two girls and two boys sharing one and my parents in the other. We also had a dog named Bob, but I can't remember where he slept!

Jim Lane

Doole's the Grocer

When I first got married I put a little order in at Doole's the grocer, opposite St Nicholas' church, once a week. Hasler, another grocer, was nearby on the corner.

Vera Howell

No Laughing

My first job was at Verdault's bakery, which was situated beside Loveday's the butchers. I learnt to be a pastry cook and earned £2 5s for a fifty-hour week. Mr Verdault was an excellent baker and scrupulously clean. He was very old-fashioned and strict, forbidding all nonsense. There was no talking, laughing or whistling allowed while we were at work.

Pat Gillen

Housego

There was a grocery shop in Guithavon Road called Housego, where I placed a regular order. We didn't have large supermarkets then, although I think there was an International in town.

Maggie Thompson

Neighbour's Errand

People would give you threepence to go down the shops. One neighbour would leave her shopping bag on the back door handle with a shopping list and 2s inside it every Thursday. After school I would get her shopping from the grocer's in Braintree Road.

Shirley Harper

Twopenn'orth of Chips

Mr Lawrence on the corner of Mill Lane and Newland Street sold fish and chips. We used to buy twopenn'orth of chips and a bottle of Tizer on our way home after a night out.

Dennis Johnson

Bridge Street Motorcycles

Don Hunt started Bridge Street Motorcycles. At the beginning he used his front room as a workshop. He sold one bike to buy another which he worked on and then resold.

John Ashcroft

The Herbalist

Mr Mottashed in Collingwood Road was a herbalist. He was an expert on the use of Pink Thermogen Wadding, which was commonly used in the treatment of chest complaints. After treatment it had to be removed in a particular way.

Mary Gillen

Calf and Box Leather

My father asked me to come into the business with him in 1958. He trained me to repair footwear. In the early days he made shoes to measure – they cost between £5 and £10 a pair, we only sold the best. They were made from soft calf leather or box leather, which we bought in rolls. They were tanned different colours; now most tanners are out of business.

John Hollick

Mr Winch's Sweet Shop

Mr Winch kept a high-class sweet shop where Lisa Marie is now. It was a narrow shop with a long counter, with quality sweets in front and ordinary ones behind. He weighed the sweets on silver scales and put them in paper bags. I would go home and count mine out and I then arranged

them on the sideboard in the kitchen – so many for each day.

Mick Horsley

Sammy Page's

Sammy Page was the man who ran the second-hand shop. It was almost opposite where the Town Hall is now; you went up steps to it. He had good quality shoes for a shilling. I bought all my cutlery from him when I first got married; in fact, he sold everything.

Ida Cunningham

Lead Line

At the Witham Bargain Centre we sold most things and our 'lead line' was a shilling pack, which consisted of a half-pound of tea – Laneco Special, a tin of condensed milk and two pounds of sugar. We used to drive up to Spitalfield in the van very early on a Monday morning to buy fruit and greengrocery.

Jim Lane

Baker on Chipping Hill

My mother's father, John Dennis, kept a little shop on Chipping Hill which later became the post office. He was a baker but he had to give the business up because people couldn't pay him. They said things like, 'I can't afford to pay you this week – one of the children needs a new pair of boots.' Of course, he still had to pay his bills,

Stables at the coal yard.

buy his flour and all that; anyway, he left and went to London.

Dennis Johnson

Among the Cobwebs

As a child I was sent on errands by my grandmother, sometimes to Mr Mottashed the chemist. We children were fascinated as he sat among the cobwebs. It was like something out of a Dickens novel.

Hilda Pluck

Coal Merchant

My father started his coal merchant business at the top of Braintree Road in 1920. This was after he came back from being a prisoner of war. He started with horses and carts and the business did really well. I've been told that at one time he stabled ten horses at No. 1 Braintree Road.

Ken Thompson

Gallant's

At the corner of Maldon Road the Gallant family started an Army Surplus store just after the war. They were eager for a sale and you could always strike a bargain with the elder Mr Gallant, whose wife was not from England. Parker Stores was at the bottom of the town and Coates' were opposite. You could get anything at old Munday's. There was a Home &

Colonial and an International Stores, and Edward Spurge who sold Irish linen.

Mick Horsley

Oscar Heddle's

Although my mother would take us to Oscar Heddle's to buy shoes and clothes, she also made us clothes. I definitely remember I wore cut-down trousers out of my father's old ones. Mother did a lot of knitting, even knitting our socks.

John Hollick

Jimmy Marshall's

My first bike during the war was made up from my granddad's old frame and then any other bits and pieces we could lay our hands on. I was fourteen years old when I got a new bike. It was a Raleigh and cost £18 1s 6d, and I got it from Jimmy Marshall's, where Allday's is now. My father paid half and I earned the rest by going fruit and vegetable picking.

John Ashcroft

Oxford Toe Caps

Over the years our customers have included Lord Stark, the old and new Lord Rayleighs who came in regularly for boot and shoe repairs. I also remember Dorothy Sayers very well. I thought her very intelligent. She was often wearing tweed plus-fours when she came in to buy her shoes. I always saw her in men's shoes; she also bought Oxford toe

caps. If you look at her statue in the town you can see she is wearing them.

John Hollick

Day-old Chicks

My father used to go to Maldon market to get some of the supplies for his shop. He would buy up the surplus crates of day-old chicks and sell them in the shop.

Jim Lane

Mr Stiff the Draper

Mr Stiff, who worked for Spurge's the drapers, was married to a French lady. He always wore a stiff winged collar of celluloid; in fact all the young lads wore grey flannels with knife-edged creases, sports coat and starched collars. If you had all this you were one of the lads.

Dennis Johnson

Uncle Ellis

Uncle Ellis sold sweet dust for a halfpenny. We would ask for sweet dust and as many pear drops as you've got, please. He always filled the cone right up to the top.

Jean Johnson

Mr Bull the Photographer

I can remember going to Mr Bull to have my photograph taken. Mrs Bull, his wife, owned what we called a 'ladies' shop'; she sold a range of clothes for both women and girls. Mrs Bull's shop was next to the George pub and her husband ran his photography business from one of the shop rooms.

Daphne LeSage

Ticky's Snacks

Before the war when I was a draper's assistant to Heddle's the tailor I used to call in a little bar called Tickey's Snacks near the corner of Maldon Road. You could buy a hot pie for threepence. It was called Tickey's because that's what we called a threepenny bit, and that is what most of the snacks cost.

Dennis Johnson

'Rocky' Markham

Mr Markham came round in a van. He made and sold rock, humbugs and toffee for a shilling a bag. Whatever you bought from him he doubled it; if you asked for threepence worth, he always gave you sixpence worth.

Pat Gillen

Percy Goodey

One of our customers at the shoe shop was Percy Goodey, a character who worked at the local gasworks – he swore a lot! His nickname was 'Ootsy', and when you was out at the pub he would try and tap you up for half a crown or five bob. I always bought

him a pint – it was cheaper as the change went back into my pocket.

John Hollick

Fifty-foot Greenhouse

My father had a greenhouse fifty foot long in which he grew tomatoes for sale. He put fine cotton across the door to prevent members of the family picking any. It didn't stop us reaching in through the windows and helping ourselves! I would describe my father as a 'Street Angel' and a 'House Devil'.

Jean Johnson

Loose Grapes

We got our fruit and vegetables from Mr Shelley, the greengrocer. At the end of the day he passed our house on his way home. He often pulled up with his horse and cart and would give us four kids the loose grapes from the bottom of the cart.

Pat Gillen

CHAPTER 6

Two World Wars

'Pop' Johnson in the First World War.

Incendiary Bombs

I was the smallest one in the fire brigade and the Germans dropped incendiary bombs all over Witham. When they fell on a roof I was the one who got pushed through the ceiling. One landed at Cuppers Farm. In the fin of the incendiary they placed the explosives, so on landing the percussion exploded the bomb and the pieces went everywhere and often stuck in the woodwork. At Collingwood Road, at Mr Gray's, there was not a rafter in the house that was not on fire, but in the end the water to put the fire out did more damage than what the bomb had done.

Fred Gaymer

Italian POW

Father rented land from the Council; it was where the sewage farm is now. During the war Italian prisoners worked on the land, pulling beet and suchlike. They were bussed there and back from their camp.

Ken Thompson

Mr Butler's Farm

I used to work at the farm; Mr Butler owned it first and then Mr Bacon took over. We chopped sugar beet, picked peas, picked up potatoes, helping with the harvest.... We used to cut sheaves and we worked from about May right through to the end of September. We pulled hock, weeded and hoed as well. The pay wasn't bad: about half a crown a day or sometimes what they called piecework. We brought our own lunch; you packed whatever you were lucky enough to have, cheese or spam, spam and more spam, sometimes boiled eggs – we were lucky as mother-in-law had some chickens. The children either came with me or stayed with mother-in-law. They were long, hot summers; if you had a thunderstorm then you had it and it was nice again. I walked to the fields with the children in the pram and started work at about 7 a.m.

Connie Edwards

Stubborn Mules

In 1914 I remember seeing soldiers in the Avenue; there were no houses there then. They were breaking in mules. The mules were very stubborn and the soldiers used to tie dummies on their backs.

Bert Baxter

Home Guard

My father-in-law was in the Home Guard and I thought it was too funny for words. Someone had to help him dress as he couldn't manage the puttees – the air was blue. He used to go down the road on his bike, tin hat swinging from the handlebars, and when he got down there and they gave him a stirrup pump, he said, 'What the heck is the good of giving me this when there's no water?' He always said he told them, 'I'll tell you something: if there's an air raid, I'm off to look after me missus first.' He was an old soldier in the First World War but was called up to the Home Guard in the Second. They met in a hall at the back of the old cycle shop where Allday's is now.

Ida Cunningham

First Reserve

My father, who had been a regular soldier, was in the First Reserve when war broke out. He heard the announcement on the wireless and had to leave immediately to be on the transport arranged; he couldn't wait for my mum to return from the shops. Only recently a lady from Glebe Crescent told me that she had seen him walking down Church Street that day. He had been so annoyed at having to leave without seeing my mother that he threw his kit bag in disgust. It landed in the garden of Mr Fenner the butcher and everything had fallen out. She said my dad had to hop over the fence and repack his bag.

Shirley Harper

Fire Brigade

During the war, Witham Council had a fire brigade the same as Chelmsford, Braintree, Colchester and Maldon, and we helped each other out. Because of the war the Government organized the Auxiliary Fire Brigade and they were based down the back of the Swan public house. There was an old council pumping station down there and the brigade moved into the old Pump House. I came back after the war and of course the Government handed all of the fire services over to the local Essex County and, true to form, all the people who'd been in the Auxiliary Service had disappeared back to their work. Well, I don't like to say this, but half of them crept in there so they didn't have to go in the Army. Old Harry Crook, Clerk of the Council, rounded up some of his Council employees – that was about half a dozen, that was the start of it.

Percy Adams

Enlisted in Witham

My father enlisted in the Army at Witham in 1940. He served in India and Burma and in 1945 he was mentioned in dispatches for bravery in the field.

Diane Watson

V2 Rockets

We had a land-girl evacuated to us. She would watch from her room which faced east, and warn us when she saw V2 rockets which had been launched in Holland. On a clear day you could see a little white wisp in

Dennis Johnson's mother and father in 1918.

the sky. If there was no bang after three minutes it was safe to leave the shelter.

John Ashcroft

Tin Hat and Silver Badge

In 1936 I joined the Air-Raid Precautions unit and got my tin hat and silver badge. When the siren went we chucked everything and went to the old police station which was being used as the unit's headquarters. I was actually in the Heavy Rescue Party. I had done a bit of first aid, so

I carried all the bandages. If a bomb dropped we tore off and shored up. Mr Adams of Adams & Mortimer was the boss.

Bert Baxter

Who Goes There?

My brother, who was a special constable, was on his way home one night when he was stopped by the ARP sentry stationed near his house. When challenged by 'Stop! Who goes there?' my brother said, 'You fool, you know who I am.' 'I know,' said the sentry, 'but I've been told to ask everyone.' Another night he knocked on a door and asked the housewife to adjust the blackout blinds. As he walked away he heard her telling her husband, 'It wasn't important: just that Poulter boy.'

Albert Poulter

The Walled Garden

Down Maldon Road there was a big building with a walled garden. I don't know quite what it was used for really, but in the First World War soldiers were billeted there – I think they were with the Warwicks. We had a couple of sergeants who lodged with us, although we only had two bedrooms. They didn't like sleeping in that place so Mother turned the front room into a bedroom for them. My parents followed the course of the war carefully and my father kept cuttings from the *Daily Telegraph* of the period.

Vera Howell

String of Eighteen

The last occasion I can remember when bombs landed in Witham was when a string of eighteen were dropped in a line from where Saxon Drive is now to Highfields Road.

John Ashcroft

Rivenhall Gliders

In 1940 I was called up. You were told to fill in a form stating where you would like to be stationed. If you put south-east England they sent you to Scotland; I ended up in

Ub Smith in 1940.

The Howell family with a First World War sergeant.

Bournemouth. I was an aircraftsman and, being a carpenter, was put on gliders at Rivenhall. They were made of wood and were inflammable; they went over to France and often got burnt out. They had three white bands painted on the fuselage so we knew they were ours. On D-Day they sent out twenty; they tried to keep it a secret and wouldn't let us out of the camp for days before. The gliders were big and held up to forty men. They could also carry jeeps and arms.

Bert Baxter

Home for a Wash

I was in the Volunteer Fire Brigade. A fortnight before war broke out we were

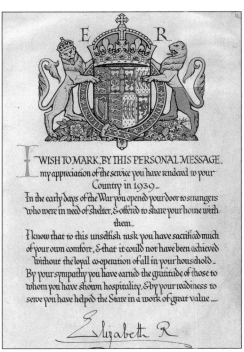

E R

I WISH TO MARK, BY THIS PERSONAL MESSAGE, my appreciation of the service you have rendered to your Country in 1939.

In the early days of the War you opened your door to strangers who were in need of shelter, & offered to share your home with them.

I know that to this unselfish task you have sacrificed much of your own comfort, & that it could not have been achieved without the loyal co-operation of all in your household.

By your sympathy you have earned the gratitude of those to whom you have shown hospitality, & by your readiness to serve you have helped the State in a work of great value.

Elizabeth R

A royal message of appreciation received after the war.

A post-war petrol coupon.

called up to do twenty-four hours a day training. There was no toilet or washroom and we cadged clothes and mattresses to go on the stone floor. Two of us slept on the ladder and one each on the footplates. We had our evening meal at the restaurant next door to what is Lloyds Bank now. On the day war was declared we were allowed to go home for a wash.

Fred Gaymer

Delivering Gas Masks

My father, George Frederick Thompson, was an ARP warden. They met in a small brick building constructed for the purpose. It was built at an angle on the corner of Chalks Road. I know my father went round Witham delivering gas masks from the back of his lorry.

Ken Thompson

The Fifth Column

One night I was sleeping in my room at the Spread Eagle when I heard a noise at the bathroom window. This was over the car park and blackout restrictions were in force, so I didn't put a light on. I saw the shadows of two people who said they were policemen. I got them to shine their torches on their badges to prove it before I opened the door. I called Mrs Hunt and went back to bed. We heard the next day that we had let the room to two fifth columnists who were signalling to the German planes from the window of their room. There was nothing in the newspaper about it.

Ida Cunningham

Perspex for Rings

A few planes came down during the war. A Tiger Moth which had run out of fuel and at least one glider landed in nearby fields. It was exciting for us children and we all dashed over. I know some people picked up Perspex which could be used to make rings.

Pat Gillen

Candy and Nylons

The GIs stationed at Rivenhall came to the dances in the Public Hall and in the hall behind the Spread Eagle. They were very generous and that's how we got candy, nylons and cigarettes like Lucky Stripes and Camel.

Ida Cunningham

Silk Parachutes

On VE Day the GIs decorated the Public Hall and put up three silk parachutes. The temptation was too much and all three disappeared quickly. I had a lovely blouse made out of my piece.

Maggie Johnson

Prisoners of War

The POWs were billeted in outhouses at the farm. They worked on one side of the field as we worked the other. They were quite a decent lot and some of them even made toys for the children. One toy I remember clearly was the 'pecking chickens'. They carved little bits of wood into bird shapes and using a badminton bat as a base, with strings attached, they pulled them up and down like pecking hens. They even managed to get a little bit of paint to finish them off. If my father-in-law were alive he would say 'they were the most polite lads imaginable.' They brought their lunch with them to the fields and had their breaks the same as us.

Connie Edwards

Compassionate Leave

My mother-in-law died suddenly in 1945 and I had to go to the police to get permission to get all her boys home. At that time one was in France, one in Germany and one in Palestine. They all came back for about a month. It was the builders Adams & Mortimer who were the undertakers up White Horse Lane.

Ida Cunningham

Anderson Shelter

The sirens used to sound when the planes passed over on their way to London. We had an Anderson shelter in the garden where the garage is now. If the children were asleep down there when the All Clear sounded, we

Jack Cunningham in November 1946.

Chalk Lane. Chipping Hill.   122996

The bombers' route to Crittall's.

would leave them till morning – they were quite cosy. We had boards to fit in the house windows for the blackout. Most people used boards, felt material or black paper.

Connie Edwards

We Saw Bombs Dropping

When I was at 56 Church Street I remember bombs falling on the meadows. They were aiming for Crittall's who produced Bailey bridges and so on for the Government. Being at Richards Yard I remember seeing a German plane more or less in line with Chalks Road. We saw bombs dropping out of the aeroplane; they were aiming at the power station in Crittall's. One hit and another hit a girder ten foot high off the floor and pushed it

out wide. It was still bent until Crittall's was demolished over forty years later.

Fred Gaymer

Junkers 88

When I was about seven or eight I remember kicking a football around in the fields behind Church Street when I saw a Junkers 88 plane swoop very low. There was no warning siren. They were coming in to bomb either Crittall's or the railway line. It was so low I saw the two pilots with their brown helmets and I looked them straight in the eye. There was a swastika on the fuselage. As it banked I ran home shouting to Mum, 'There's a German plane!' All she said was, 'Don't frighten Mrs Brown next door.' We heard that Mr Edgington of the Home Guard took a pot-shot at it as it flew over. Someone said that was a silly thing to do as they might come back for revenge.

Pat Gillen

Lucky Fossil

I had a close call during the war. Two German planes came over very low and blew me right off my feet. As I got up I found I was holding a fossil. I've never let it out of my sight since: I carry it everywhere, and have done since that day in 1940. My wife says it wears holes in my pockets.

Dennis Johnson

Army Officers

During the war there were always staff shortages and I was often called to give a hand in the kitchen at the Spread Eagle in the evening when the maids had a night off. I loved it when Chef asked me to beard the mussels; I was crazy about shellfish and used to sample them often. I also helped the housemaid and was even asked to make tea and toast for the army officers' breakfasts. They were often billeted in the pub. Unfortunately they were used to giving orders and I had to remind them that I was doing them a favour. In the end we got on well.

Ida Cunningham

Wounded at Arras

Father served in the 9th Essex in the First World War. He was wounded at Arras prior to capture by the Germans. Mother received two telegrams, the first about his being wounded and the second about his capture. He returned home for Christmas 1918.

Ken Thompson

Mr Redmond's Shutters

On VE Day they lit a big bonfire in the High Street. Mr Redmond, who had an antique shop where Woolworth's is now, had ancient and unusual bay windows. He put his shutters up and stood on guard all evening. At 10.30 p.m. he thought it would be safe to go in for a quick drink but when he came out the shutters were burning on the bonfire.

Dennis Johnson

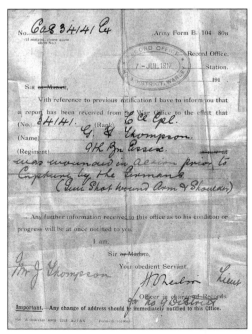

A War Office communication.

The Church Street party on VE Day.

Ruby from Lowestoft

Evacuees – don't remind me – my first experience was terrible, a horrible woman and her two children from London. Then we got a nice couple from Scotland. He was in the RAF and worked at the Drome at Rivenhall and his wife worked at Sorrell's the butchers. Then we got a couple of nice chaps from Ipswich and then finally Ruby from Lowestoft. She was the life and soul of the party, she loved the kids and we loved her. She asked Reg to give her away when she got married, and she married from this house.

Connie Edwards

£100 Gratuity

My father Jack, who had been a regular soldier, was recalled when war was declared.

He served for six years as batman to one of the officers. On discharge he was given £100 gratuity.

John Hollick

Never Mind Hitler!

On the journey to school in Chelmsford there were often air raids. The bus stopped and we all dived for cover. People's faith was strong then and they said, 'Never mind Hitler, let's get on with it.'

Pat Gillen

Shared Coupons

My mother told us that during rationing, clothing coupons had to go a long way.

Most people made their own clothes and families normally shared coupons. Shoes cost around 3s 6d and a coat and frock one guinea.

Diane Watson

The Essex

I was conscripted into the Army and went to Horley Barracks before I finished up in Italy. I was in the Essex and transferred to the Service Corps.

Percy Adams

VE Day

We knew something was happening. We were waiting on tenterhooks and had our wireless on and hung about chatting to the neighbours. Dad was home on leave and we went down to the town. Everybody went to town and got together singing and dancing in the street. It was a long night, I'll not forget it. Everyone in the street brought a table or a chair, and everyone brought a plate of food. Where they got the stuff from, the Lord only knows – there was even jelly, after all those years of rationing.

Connie Edwards

Dogfight

One sunny Saturday afternoon my sister and I were cutting cabbages in the garden when German planes came over and there was a dogfight above our heads. My father

yelled 'Take cover!' I went in the shed but my sister stood in the middle of the greenhouse.

Jean Johnson

Blackshirts

When the Army was posted all round Witham there were no raids. Within twenty-four hours of them moving out the bombers were back. The gossip was that the Blackshirts had informed the enemy of the Army's movements.

John Ashcroft

Extra Rations

My father-in-law, who was Ted Cunningham the local butcher, told me some tales. He was very well known in Witham for squeezing the rations and giving that little bit extra. That shop was almost opposite the Spread Eagle and is now a charity shop.

Ida Cunningham

GI Gum

When I was playing in the coal yard opposite Witham railway station as a young lad, we would see two or three lorries arriving to pick up GIs from the station. We would cadge what we could because they had more than we did. They were friendly and usually gave us pieces of chewing gum.

Ken Thompson

Emily Bibby at Cooper Taber during the First World War.

Emily Bibby

My mother Emily Bibby worked at Cooper Taber during the First World War when it was conscripted to produce munitions. When we were children, after the First War, we had to go to the Cenotaph on Poppy Day. There was a terrific parade – the Scouts, Guides and everybody you could think of. We used to end up at the Congregational church. The club which was at the front of it burned down but that was before my time.

Percy Adams

Lost His Courage

My uncle was a Squadron Leader in the RAF. He was 20 stone and 6ft 4ins tall. At the outbreak of war he taught Australian Spitfire pilots. He came to see his family in Witham and stayed with us. He had heard about the Doodlebugs and told us he was keen to see one. When the siren went off and the Doodlebug engine cut out he lost his courage and in his rush to get into the Anderson shelter he cut his bald head.

John Ashcroft

CHAPTER 7

Fashion Tips

Velvet dresses.

Royal Blue Velvet

Once my mother sent to Barker's in Kensington for some royal blue velvet material. She asked Miss Robinson, a Witham seamstress, to make me a dress out of it. I hated the measuring up but she made a lovely dress and finished it off with a lace collar and cuffs. Miss Robinson worked in a cottage between the haberdashery shop, where Motormania is now, and Keith's sweet shop. One day when I should have been at Sunday school I went climbing trees in that new dress and split the skirt all up the back.

Hilda Pluck

Dennis Johnson's grandmother.

Liberty Bodices

We wore vests, liberty bodices and petticoats with drawers – that's what we called them in those days – and the drawers buttoned onto the liberty bodice, which was shop-bought. Mother made everything else; they were normally made out of cotton or flannelette and we always wore a vest, even in summer.

Vera Howell

Prams

The pram was built for twins and if it rained, with both hoods up I had to peer round the handles to see where I was going. Luckily I've got a good sense of humour. I'd say to people, 'if you see a big pram coming along with nobody pushing it, you'll find me under the handles.'

Ida Cunningham

Port and Lemon

My dad drank with Alf Good in the Red Lion. The pub shut at ten and my dad would fetch Mum to have her drink of port and lemon at ten to ten. Of course, in those days respectable women didn't go to the pub for the whole evening and never entered one on their own.

Jim Lane

Early Recycling

We were lucky. Mother-in-law was a very good needlewoman: she could take something to pieces, turn it and remake it. Really, she was a very clever woman and she could make anything. I also did a lot of knitting so the kids were always smartly turned out.

Connie Edwards

Elephant Crêpe

My wife's wedding dress, they said, was made out of elephant crêpe. I never knew what that was and still don't!

Bert Baxter

Kilts

Mother made the family's clothes on a hand sewing machine. I usually wore dresses that were fairly plain. I do remember sometimes having a kilt and a nice jumper. Mother brought the material from the Co-op in the High Street; they also sold millinery items.

Vera Howell

Hand Machines

I made most of my clothes on a hand sewing machine. I bought the material from Cooper-Cocks up the town. Dressmaking as well as reading and dancing were my main hobbies.

Margaret Brannan

Jolly Rich

You were jolly rich if you had lisle stockings. Stockings were always made from material you could darn – mending and darning were the normal things to do if clothing got torn. We didn't have nylons but I remember when tights first appeared in the shops. It took a year for Reg to persuade me to wear them. He was the one who went out to buy the first pair to make sure I wore 'em. He was right – I never went back to stockings.

Connie Edwards

An American Suit

We got married in 1955 at Bethel Chapel in Church Street. I wore a lovely pink-coloured suit. My aunt, Mrs Richardson, who had been visiting relatives in America, brought it back for me. Pastor Swift conducted the ceremony.

Rose Willshire

Turbans

I remember women wearing turbans. I think the fashion started when female workers in shops and factories needed to keep their hair out of the machinery. They wound a long scarf round their heads, probably made out of cotton or a silky material.

Shirley Harper

Fred and Rose Willshire on their wedding day in 1955.

Ida Cunningham aged twenty-one in 1944.

Dog Collars

In 1946 when I joined the Force we still wore dog collars. After a couple of years they introduced collars and ties. Surprisingly, a lot of constables were reluctant to change.

Ron Shayshutt

Princess Margaret Rose

I had a brother and three sisters. Being the youngest, all I got was hand-me-downs, though I always had new clothes for Sunday school – I wore white ankle socks with black patent shoes with a strap. I can always remember my mother having a dress made for us girls in the same style as Princess Margaret Rose's. It was ever so pretty, with a pink background covered in little flowers.

Jean Johnson

Hand-sewn Shoes

I wore berets and bonnets when I was small and once I had a tam-o'-shanter. I had button boots which you did up with a special button hook. My husband's father was a cobbler and made some wonderful hand-sewn shoes.

Hilda Pluck

Velvet in Winter

I remember having a dark red overcoat that Mother made. We always had a hat – straw in summer and a velvet or material type in winter.

Vera Howell

Coupons

It was terribly awkward to get anything, clothes especially, during rationing. Luckily I had five brothers and borrowed some of their coupons. My mother made my uniform, which was a plain pale green dress and white apron with black shoes and a navy coat.

Ida Cunningham

Grey Winter Coat

Mrs Hammond in Easton Road made me a lovely winter coat out of a grey army blanket. We did all sorts of things using different types of material during the years of rationing.

Jean Johnson

Outworkers

Most girls who left school went to Pinkham's glove factory. They also had outworkers for embroidery and sewing on buttons. They were beautiful gloves made of all sorts of fabrics. If you went anywhere you always wore gloves.

Shirley Harper

The Cobbler

The shoes were hard. I don't know what they were made of – you had a job to get them and when you did they didn't last long. We took them to Mr Charlie Poulter, the cobbler in Cressing Road. He was very good and mended them whenever possible. Those ration coupons came into it every time – if you hadn't got the coupons you couldn't get anything.

Connie Edwards

Modes

There used to be a shop, I think it was called Modes, next to the George pub. I bought a lot of clothes there. I particularly remember a black taffeta skirt which was very fashionable and I liked it very much.

Pat Taylor

Fox Furs

Smart women like my mother and sisters who followed fashion had real fox furs with the head and claws which they wore round their necks. They always wore a hat and often it was felt cloche. My sister Beattie would see a fashionable design and make her own paper pattern from which she would cut and sew. The finished

Beatrice Clare Dennis aged two and a half years.

Fred Gaymer's sisters.

article was always very smart and up to date.

Jim Lane

Fichu with Beads

One of the Miss Luards wore a fichu, a stiff lace collar with beads on each point. When I was little I remember sitting in church and being worried – petrified – as I thought they were nails and would stick in her neck if she moved her head.

Jean Johnson

New for Easter

My mother made a lot of my clothes. I had younger twin sisters and we all had everything new for Easter.

Daphne LeSage

Maternity Dresses

The Misses Luard ran a scheme where pregnant ladies could borrow maternity dresses. After the child was born, they collected and cleaned the dresses before loaning them out to somebody else.

Albert Poulter

Little Grey Fur Collar

My husband-to-be, Stanley, who came from Sheringham, brought a selection of engagement rings for me to choose from. We married at All Saints' church in 1935 and I wore a blue *crêpe de chine* dress and a pink wide-brimmed straw hat. After my wedding I changed into a new grey coat with a little fur collar. We caught the train to London before going by coach to Hampshire for a week.

Vera Howell

Ballerina-length Dress

I got married in St Nicholas' church in 1958. Mr Black was the minister. I wore a ballerina-length dress, which was fashionable then. It was made out of lace and I had a three-quarter veil and pearl headdress which I had bought in London. Rina Shelley, Pat Butler and my sister-in-law Maureen were my bridesmaids.

Shirley Harper

Curling Tongs

When I wanted to curl my hair, sometimes my mother used rags and sometimes metal tongs. She heated the tongs over a flame, probably the hob on the gas cooker, then catching a piece of hair she twisted it and held the tongs in place until they were cold. It was necessary to reheat the tongs for every tress that was curled. You could feel the heat and hear the sizzle as your hair got burnt into shape.

Jean Johnson

Sunday best.

Albert Gaymer in his trilby.

Trilby and Cap

My father Albert, like most men, always wore a hat. He had a trilby for special events and for when the weather was better. For everyday wear and working days on the land he wore a cap.

Fred Gaymer

Black Market

I got a costume off a friend, who knew a friend who knew someone. Lots of people had to buy things that way during the war years. It was navy blue, tailored, a good quality material and it cost me about 10s.

Ida Cunningham

Mother's Hat

My mother usually wore a hat. One of her favourites was a small, darkish straw hat with tiny holes. Her hat pins normally had little black knobs on the ends. She used to meet me out of Sunday school and we would go to the church service. I hated this because we had to kneel on something similar to rough coconut matting. My aunt used to knit me cotton socks that had little holes in the pattern and they dug in my legs when I knelt down on the matting.

Vera Howell

Reach-me-downs

When I was fourteen I had my first pair of long trousers. They were reach-me-downs from my brother – most of our clothes were 'make do and mend'. Across the road from us was a Mr Garrett, a tailor. Mother had bought some cloth, it was a bargain. She was furious with Mr Garrett because he had cut the suit short. He only just made the suit so I reckon she only just paid him.

Albert Poulter

Father Wilson

We were married at the church of the Holy Family by Father Wilson. I wore a dress of Irish lace with a satin train. Our honeymoon was spent in Ireland.

Mary Gillen

Teddy Boys

I liked the idea of being a Teddy Boy. I had a DA and a Tony Curtis quiff with sideburns. I wore the narrowest trousers I could get hold of and later on I remember wearing a duffel coat.

Ken Smith

Double String of Pearls

We got married in 1953. I've still got my wedding dress which was cotton overlaid with lace. It had a long train and I bought it in Southend. It was nothing elaborate – we didn't have much money in those days. I wore a double string of pearls bought by my husband, Dennis. He wore a blue woollen suit which cost either £3 or £4 from Mr Macleod, a Braintree bespoke tailor.

Jean Johnson

1940s hairstyle.

Father Burn, parish priest from 1940 to 1954.

A Smart Man

As well as managing Ripon's tobacco wholesalers, my husband Stanley used to travel a bit and get orders from other shops. He was always a smart man and usually wore a navy blue suit and crisp white shirt.

Vera Howell

Bath Chair

I remember seeing a woman in a bath chair. She was being drew up the High Street by a man who walked in front. Bath chairs were often made out of willow osiers like they make baskets with. Three wheels, the one at the front was connected to a long handle, so if you pushed the chair the person sitting could steer, or you could swivel it round and use the handle to pull it.

Fred Gaymer

Sugar Water

We couldn't afford a hairdresser in those days. We grew our hair long and rolled it round a stocking. We girls often used sugar water to set our hair.

Ida Cunningham

White Satin

We were married in 1951 in the old Catholic church by Father Burn. The lady next door, Mrs Oakley, who was a seamstress, made my wedding dress; it was white satin. The three bridesmaids wore white and pink. We went to Ireland for our honeymoon.

Eileen Smith

CHAPTER 8

Travelling

Dusty roads in Witham.

Oliver Cromwell

In the 1950s when the train engine was called *Oliver Cromwell* certain firemen and drivers would take us on the footplate as far as Chelmsford. We came back to Witham in the guard's van on any train we were lucky enough to get.

Pat Gillen

Three Bus Companies

There were three main bus companies operating in Witham: Moores, Eastern National and Hicks Bros. It was 1s 3d for a return ticket to Chelmsford and 1s 6d if you went to Colchester.

Pat Smith

Mill Beach

My grandfather had a pony and cart and he sometimes took me brother and I for a ride on Sunday afternoon to Mill Beach. When we got there the pony was taken out of the cart and tied up in one of the stables along with other ponies. Sometimes there were several people with ponies and carts as Mill Beach was a popular local attraction. There were always a lot of cyclists and people who had walked, but never a motor car those days. These trips were arranged when it was high tide at Maldon. Sometimes we were able to paddle; if not, we sat by the sea watching the boats.

Fred Gaymer

Crab and Winkle

Carnival day in Maldon was always the first Monday in August. We used to pay ninepence return on the 'Crab and Winkle' which was always crowded on Carnival Day. We normally stayed for the firework display on the lake and got back to Witham at about 10.30. They used to run excursion trains to Clacton and Southend to see the lights on a Saturday night. These trips, which cost 1s 6d, always drew a good crowd.

Dennis Johnson

Cycle Master

I had a Cycle Master, which was a bit like a moped. You bought the unit for about £12 and had it attached to the wheel of your ordinary bike. Dick Ashley had a garage in Hatfield Road and he fitted mine. I got my first car in 1967. It was a Reliant Robin and cost me £665 new.

Fred Willshire

Mr Chalk the Taxi Driver

There were three taxis in town, a 24-hour one in Collingwood Road, Mr Capwood just past the police station and Mr Chalk from Crossroads. He plied his trade from the railway station and always wore a suit and tie and a peaked cap. If he had a fare he didn't acknowledge you, because once he'd put his peaked cap on we knew he was in business; if his cap was off he would give you a friendly wave. It was a fair-sized vehicle with a glass partition that slid behind the driver. When Mr Chalk had no customers we would see him cleaning and shining his car.

Mick Horsley

Austin

Pete bought his first car in 1958. It was not a new one and cost him about £10.

Margaret Brannan

Mr George Cook

My mother's brother George Cook used his horse and cart to run a carrier business between Hatfield Peverel and Witham. It was like an early Parcelforce – for a few pence he would make local deliveries. He also undertook purchases for those unable to make them themselves, especially cumbersome or heavy items like horse feed or tools. He normally had a set route which everyone knew and was probably available on each route a couple of times a week.

Fred Gaymer

My £7 Bike

I cycled to work every day on the bike my dad bought me from E.G. Coates. It cost him about £7 I think. I really got a lot of wear out of that bike and cycled to Maldon in the holidays. My uncle had a big house there and I helped him by working with the pigs he kept in the orchard. I had many happy times at my uncle's house.

Ken Smith

Train Smash

Each time a train was due a bell sounded in my grandmother's house and she went out and opened the crossing gate. One Sunday morning the bell didn't ring and the Braintree to Clacton excursion train smashed the gates to pieces. Fortunately no-one was hurt.

Dennis Johnson

Carrier's Cart

I don't remember my grandparents. My sister did and she remembers going with a cousin to the funeral of one of them in Rivenhall. They wore identical little grey costumes and got a ride in a carrier's cart from Witham to Rivenhall.

Vera Howell

Dusty Roads

Most roads were very dusty, even in town. In the warm weather they were sprayed with water to stop the dust blowing about. This spraying was carried out by the man driving a horse-drawn cart with a large tank and spray bar fitted on the frame. The driver filled the tank from a fire hydrant and when he pulled a lever the water sprayed from the spray bar at the back of the cart as the horse walked forward. The whole of Newland Street from the Catholic church, Bridge Street and parts of Hatfield Road, Mill Lane, Guithavon Street, Maldon Road, Collingwood Road and Avenue Road – all these highways were sometimes sprayed twice a day. The driver had to fill up the tank several times.

Fred Gaymer

Sense of Freedom

My bike gave me a lovely sense of freedom. On Sundays with friends I cycled all over the place, right round Rivenhall, Silver End, Braintree and finally looping back through Cressing into Witham. Sometimes we would be singing our heads off, especially with songs like 'June is busting out all over' and 'Oh what a beautiful morning'.

Shirley Harper

Station Bridge

The railway bridge is now a lot wider than it used to be. Double-decker buses would scrape the wall as they turned into Braintree Road. Mr Ross's cabin which sold sweets and things was on the bridge next to the old cattle market. It was scary when they widened the bridge because for a short while there was no wall between the road and the drop onto the railway line.

Mick Horsley

90 Miles Per Hour

One of the many lodgers we had worked as a traveller and his headquarters were in Cambridge. He owned a Norton motorbike; I remember speeding on it at 90mph. My stomach was in my mouth. At this time petrol was 2s a gallon.

Albert Poulter

Driving Lessons

I had driving lessons from Mr Russell, a very patient man. They cost 14s 6d for 45 minutes and I passed my test the second time I took it.

Ken Smith

I Pushed Him Miles

My brother was three years older than me. He was an apprentice motor mechanic at what used to be the West End garage in Witham. He used to repair motorbikes for different people, privately as well as at business. He had motorbikes that you had to push and then jump on; you had to push it fast enough to start the engine, then jump on. I must have pushed him miles over the years. I used to say you've got to be pretty quick to manage it.

Fred Gaymer

Puffing Billy

Mr Birch worked on the railway. During the war his wife would send me to him with a

A rare outing by car.

shepherd's pie covered by a cloth for his dinner. I took it to Witham station, got on the 'Puffing Billy' and delivered it to him at the signal box at White Notley where he worked. I then stayed with Mr Birch for the rest of the day.

Pat Gillen

Various Carts

When I was young there were many horses and carts, and ponies and small carts for the delivery of milk, bread and meat. The milkman came round twice a day. There were larger horses for carting coal from the goods station to people's houses and the gas works; it was a common sight to see big horses carting wood and other heavy goods around Witham.

Fred Gaymer

Two-stroke Bikes

On rural beats we used bikes first, then two-stroke motorbikes, later to be followed by small vans and finally cars. I remember a young PC who complained his motorbike was not powerful enough to get up Wickham Bishops hill. I think he was after four wheels.

Ron Shayshutt

Jimmy Quilter

Jimmy Quilter, my great-grandfather, was an odd job man. He went to Chelmsford with his donkey and cart. The well-trained donkey turned into the Duke of Wellington on his way back with no command from my great-grandfather. Jimmy Quilter liked his drink over-much and my great-grandmother had been heard to reply to the question, 'Can I borrow Jimmy's ladder?' 'No, he's swallowed it.'

Dennis Johnson

Swift Saloon

My uncle often spoke of the first car he remembered seeing. It was a big black saloon called a Swift, a six-seater with a hood that rolled back like a pram hood. There were wide running boards and carriage lamps on the side. A starting handle was used to get it going; after a certain distance it had to be started again. The driver stuck his arm out to turn right, his passenger to turn left. There were rubber hooters on either side. The windows were Perspex and the seats Rexine.

Diane Watson

Braintree Bridge

The Braintree Road bridge had to be widened as the path was so narrow you couldn't push a pram along it. An interesting feature was that the kerb had been made from metal railway tracks. All the kerbs further up the Braintree Road had to be lowered to enable two vehicles to pass each other.

Mick Horsley

George Cook's carrier business.

Bygone Stations

I don't remember going on holiday much, just the odd school day-trip to Walton. My mother would take us on the 'Crab and Winkle' to Maldon for a day's outing. The train picked up passengers from Wickham Bishops and Ulting on the way. Both those places had stations then.

John Hollick

Maintenance Work

As a result of the maintenance neglect during the war years, which was followed by the big freeze of 1946/47, the railways were unable to deliver coal to the factories. Crittall's couldn't shift any windows and to keep the workforce occupied they took on repair work on the railway wagons.

Pat Smith

No Gears

My grandfather liked cycling. The Avenue was a quarter of a mile long and a straight road so Grandfather and his friends used it to race up and down on their cycles. I got my first bike just before the war. My father bought me a new one and it cost him £3 19s. There was no way he could afford that so like everybody else he paid weekly. It was a very basic machine and of course didn't have any gears.

Dennis Johnson

Two-bob Excursion

The railways ran an excursion train between Braintree and London. It was about 2s for a return ticket. I visited my brother in 1921 and I think the highlight of the trip was riding on the trams.

Albert Poulter

Motor Cars

There were only about six people in the Witham area who owned motor cars, so in those days we were lucky to see one, and everyone stopped when they heard a strange noise. Motor cars were only allowed to travel slowly in the town. The speed limit was 10mph and this wasn't changed until 1931.

Fred Gaymer

Peterborough Express

Johnny Mason came to school after doing his paper round and told us that he had seen the Peterborough Express plough into the back of a goods van at the crossing. We later learnt that Mr Bull the guard, who lived in Cressing Road, was killed. It was doubly tragic because he had swapped duties to do someone a favour. They took the steam engine and metal bogies away but burnt the wooden carriages in the farmer's field.

Mick Horsley

Rattle

I had my first bike when I was about twelve. It belonged to my friend Shirley

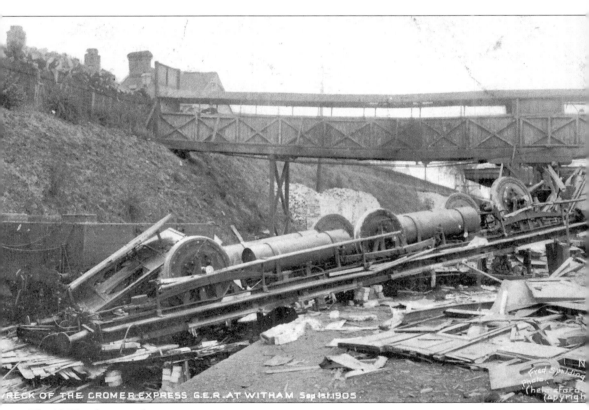

The 1905 railway crash.

Brannan; I paid her 15s for it after she had got a new one. It rattled a bit but it got me where I wanted to go and I rode it until the day I got married.

Shirley Harper

Queen Wilhelmina

My mum had a bike called a Queen Wilhelmina; we all rode it. It weighed a ton and had strips over the wheel and a guard over the chain to protect your clothes.

Jean Johnson

Racing Foals

Mr Bryce at Little Braxted bred racehorses. When the foals were brought to Witham station the chief groom walked in front of them, right down the middle of the road, waving his stick with a knob on it. He led the horses to the pens behind the goods yard before they were loaded onto trains and taken to Newmarket.

Percy Adams

Royal Mail Van

Motts Lane crossing was one of the Royal Mail pickup points. It was always interesting to watch the chute come out from the mail van and pull in the mailbags as the train went by. Further up the line the incoming mail was deposited for the waiting postmen to carry up the bank.

Mick Horsley

Hillman Minx

It took us five years for us to save for our first motor car. It was a Hillman Minx 1500 and cost £675. I bought it from Rowley's of Witham.

Ken Thompson

Accident in Malting Lane

I bought a motorbike in 1956, a BSA 250, and promptly crashed it in Maltings Lane. I was going as fast as I could, without the experience to handle it, and I broke my leg in eleven places. When I recovered I got back on the bike, which had been repaired, and rode it for the next two years without any mishap. As a young man I paid 3s 7d a gallon for petrol and would drive to Dover and back for £1 10s.

John Ashcroft

Austin Seven

My first car was an Austin Seven. I bought it in the thirties. It cost £45 and petrol was 1s a gallon.

Percy Adams

Harley Davidson

I was very friendly with Dan Crittall. He had a Harley Davidson with a sidecar and often took five or six of us out for a spin on it.

Percy Adams

Pop Johnson as a young man.

A Christmas to Remember

Christmas Eve 1948 or 1949, the gatekeepers on the Braintree line had a present they would never forget. A quick-witted driver managed to stop his runaway steam engine just before it reached the crossing-house door.

Mick Horsley

Strutt's Bride

The Hon. Charles Strutt – I remember him taken in his brougham every morning. You'd see him go by on his way to business and then again at night when they picked him up from the station. He got married late in his life and my uncle Bob was farm manager for him. He organized all his employees to be at the station with this horse-drawn cart. They picked up him and his bride who were then pulled home to Blunts Hall. My uncle Bob was good at organizing and did things right.

Fred Gaymer

First Bike for £5

We all cycled everywhere. I bought my first bike at Norton's in Dublin for £5 and it cost me 5s to bring it across to Witham. You could get a decent second-hand bike for £1 at that time.

Pat Smith

Bus to Work

I met Fred on the bus when we both worked at Black Notley. I caught the bus at the White Horse, Chipping Hill, and Fred got on later at Highfields.

Rose Willshire

Sugar Beet Trains

The railway banks were well cared for, with growth cut back as any sparks from the steam engines could have started a fire. When the wind blew up our garden the smuts would make the washing dirty and my mother would say, 'That blooming train', but at weekends in September it was interesting to stand at the bottom of the garden and watch the sugar beet trains go back and forth to Felsted.

Mick Horsley

Ladies' Bikes

A ladies' bike cost about £2 1s 3d. My girlfriend, who was at that time a housemaid at Terling Place, bought one and paid for it at about half a crown a week. I think she bought it brand new from Glovers.

Fred Gaymer

CHAPTER 9

A Miscellany

Royal visitors: King George V and Queen Mary.

Royalty Passing By

My father worked at Bill Newman's dairy, near where the Bramston swimming pool is today. One morning when my father let all the cows out to cross the road and go up to the fields he was severely told off by the police because the herd blocked the road just as King George V and Queen Mary were passing through Witham in their Daimler. Although there were gangs of police around, nobody had told the people of Witham that royalty would be passing by.

Percy Adams

Oxygen Cylinder

I remember visiting my aunt and uncle who lived in a prefab in Church Street. My aunt suffered from chronic asthma and always had a huge oxygen cylinder next to her bed.

Diane Watson

The Misses Luard's Scheme

We used to pay in a scheme run by the Misses Luard. We paid a very meagre amount for maternity care, about a shilling a month, I think it was, to the Misses Luard. They ran the nursing home. I had my first two children there. You know that bungalow in Collingwood Road next door to what used to be Heddle's the bespoke tailors, well that was the nursing home then. I had the other four at home and the sisters took it in turns to come out and tend to me and the baby at home.

Connie Edwards

The Snowdons

I went to Sunday school at the Bethel Chapel from the age of four. The teachers were Mr and Mrs Snowdon. Mrs Snowdon came from Scotland but Mr Snowdon was a local man. His mother lived in a little cottage down Moat Farm Chase and she had a peg leg. It was a rough track and I shall never know how she got up such a steep slope, but she managed it somehow. Mr and Mrs Snowdon lived near us and were very gentle characters.

Shirley Harper

The slope at Moats Farm Chase.

The Colonel

My father was commonly known as 'the Colonel'. When he was a youngster they played soldiers and he always wanted to be in charge. The name stuck: his mail was addressed to 'the Colonel' and even his doctor called him that! In fact he was a sergeant who served in World War I.

Jean Johnson

Greyhounds for £4

Alf Good, who had a little garage workshop behind the Co-op, also bred greyhounds. He sold them for £4 each. Out of one litter he gave my father the runt. The poor thing had a bad leg and caught distemper and soon died. We would go to Southend dog track which had just opened; it was 1s 3d to go in the cheap bit and 2s for the elite section.

Jim Lane

Jug and Bottle

When my granddad was working in Church Street my mother took me to the Jug and Bottle at the Woolpack pub. I handed my jug over the counter and got two pints of Daniels 4X Strong Ale, which he had with his dinner. It only cost a few pence a pint.

John Ashcroft

Carlos the Dog

I discovered why Carlos the Great Dane growled at the police. He often lay outside the hotel on the pavement and as the policeman passed he gave him a friendly pat on the head with his glove. I was later told that in those days some policemen put a marble in the finger of the glove to give a warning to any naughty boy who misbehaved. If that's true, it would explain the dog's behaviour towards policemen.

Ida Cunningham

Witham Bench

When my father, Ub Smith, was demobbed, he returned to his job as an accountant with Lord Rayleigh's estate, and we lived by turn in Great Leighs, Terling and Hatfield Peverel. He served as a Justice of the Peace on the Witham Bench during the sixties and until his early death in 1970.

Diane Watson

The Commission Agent

My father, George Smith, worked for the railway company before becoming a bookie. He conducted his business from our home. I know his runners got caught and were run in once or twice. The bookies' runners were given a leather bag with a round top which had a clock in it. My father knew what time the bag was sealed because the clock stopped – that way he knew all the bets were in the bag before the race was run. They got caught by the police once or twice and had the bag confiscated, but my father always bailed them out. Of course, it was illegal to gamble in those days.

Jean Johnson

117

Ub Smith during the sixties.

Father Burn

Father Burn, who lived at the Presbytery next to the old Catholic church, was a very kind and gentle man, totally dedicated to his calling. Many Witham families benefited from his acts of generosity.

Pat Gillen

National Service

I was called up to do my National Service on 4 September 1952. At one point I was on the Isle of Wight when there was a prison revolt there. We were called in to prevent them escaping. Ron Woods, who lived in Hatfield Road, was in the same regiment as me and was also on the Isle of Wight.

Ken Thompson

Dodman's Parrot

Mr Dodman's sister came to live with him and she would come to the front gate with a parrot on her shoulder. All the kids would gather round, as you never saw parrots in those days.

Shirley Harper

Water Hole

If you go down by the riverside off Bridge Street, just past the bridge, you'll see where it's hollowed out. That's where the cattle used to come down from Howbridge Farm and walk into the river.

Percy Adams

A Good Grin

What I think is an asset, a big asset, and whenever I am asked how to be a nonagenarian, I tell them a good grin is a great help. For example, one of the things that always makes me smile is my first shave. When I was fifteen my brother said, 'Come here and I will shave you.' He used a German-type open razor and whatever soap the family happened to be using at the time. Another brother was very keen on poetry, but the lads thought Shakespeare was too long, so we became known as the 'Shaker' Poulters. Someone else who got a nickname in a funny way was Mr Thompson. A man, a stranger in Witham, went into the Albert pub looking for Mr Thompson. This man stuttered and asked for 'To-To-Totie', and that is how Totie Thompson got his name.

Albert Poulter

Mr Randall's Thresher

Mr Randall had a traction engine which he hired out for threshing in the fields. We boys would chase after it and hang off the back to get a ride as it was being moved from place to place. If we got caught we'd get a hard clump. Lots of times we would see Mr Randall's traction engine outside the Cherry Tree. Wisps of smoke would come out of the chimney whilst I suppose the driver was getting stoked up inside the pub.

Pat Gillen

In for a Long Stay

Mrs De'ath, a one-time landlady of the Woolpack, was a chatterbox. When she put her elbows on the bar, you knew she was getting ready to talk to you and you were in for a long stay. I nearly packed up drinking when it went up to a shilling a pint in the fifties.

John Ashcroft

Laying on of Hands

My grandfather, George Smith, would carry out 'the laying on of hands', or healing as it is now called. My mother, who was very sceptical, was anxious to rid herself of small warts on her finger; her father-in-law healed them, much to her astonishment. Sadly he did not believe in the medical profession

and died many years before his time from a common and minor complaint. He refused medical help, believing it was God's will whether he lived or died.

Diane Watson

Witham Fire Brigade

I was in the Witham fire brigade from 1947 and served in it for the next ten years.

Bert Baxter

The Lemon Prize

When food was rationed I remember going to a dance at the Public Hall where I won the raffle prize. It was a lemon and I became

Albert Poulter, aged ninety-two years.

Bert Baxter in the fire brigade.

Fred and Albert Gaymer with Mr Weevis and Mr Butcher.

Fred and Albert with the horse hoe.

the most popular girl in the hall. Fruit was so scarce they all wanted that lemon, but I saved it and took it home for my mum.

Jean Johnson

Discharge Papers

When I was discharged from the armed forces in 1946 I was given fifty-six days' pay, and with my Discharge Papers a book containing a travel warrant in case I was called back.

Pat Smith

Spanish Flu

I got the Spanish flu in 1918 – it was a big epidemic. Some families lost more than one member. There were four or five of the Wisemans that were lost; you can see their stones if you go to the cemetery. I was very ill for a while, often delirious so that I wandered out of the house.

Bert Baxter

£2 Boot Allowance

In Witham there was myself and another woman police special. We felt unpopular with the regular officers. It was all voluntary although we did get a monthly boot allowance. The amount depended on how many hours you had worked. It generally worked out to about £2 per month. We were also issued with whistles which operated within our limited range of duties.

Maureen Scollan

Self-taught

My mother hadn't received any proper education, really, but she taught herself to read and write. People would come to our door to get her to write their important notes or to fill in forms. She was marvellous – she even wrote poetry.

Vera Howell

Town Flood

In 1947 when the heavy snows thawed, the River Brain flooded parts of Witham up to 20 or 30ft either side of its banks. It flooded under the railway arch in Armond Road and

Inspector Maureen Scollan.

across the town dump. I tried to cycle through but fell off and got soaked. I then went to the forge to try and dry off in front of the fire before going home, but a neighbour saw me and told my mother, so I was in trouble again anyway.

John Ashcroft

Women's Vote

It was in 1928 when all women finally got the right to vote. I think my mother felt that women had achieved something important.

Fred Gaymer

Mr Dodman the Sweep

Old Mr Dodman was a chimney sweep. Superstitious people thought that chimney sweeps brought them good luck and he used to advertise himself, for weddings and such, in the cinema – that's when seats cost 9d. His wife, little Mrs Dodman, was a dear.

Hilda Pluck

Lord Braintree

Valentine Crittall was the first Labour MP to represent the Witham area. Crittall's factory provided a lot of employment in Witham and nearly every window down Cressing Road showed a poster saying 'Vote for Crittall'. He was soon elevated to Lord Braintree.

Albert Poulter

Childhood Ambitions

I had grown up next door to the police house in Silver End and always wanted to be a policewoman. I started as a special constable at Witham. It is strange that Essex was one of the first counties to set up a police force but one of the last to employ women as police officers. I remember my first morning at the station. When I walked into the locker room there was a big poster of a naked man on the wall. The old sergeant was more upset than I was about it. I had to fight to walk the beat, as a woman; they wanted to protect me.

Maureen Scollan

Green Moustache

When I joined the Girls' Training Corps Miss Lucy Croxall was the person in charge. We regularly went on church parades marching through Witham on our way to the church. On one of these parades the pastor officiating at St Nicholas' was a locum. He was a tiny man who couldn't see above the lectern. We all giggled at this and Miss Croxall who was sitting in the row behind poked us in the back. My friend had green astrakhan gloves and she stuffed one in her mouth to try and stop herself laughing. The dye from the glove ran and she ended up with a green moustache. She had to finish the parade wearing her green moustache and we laughed all the way back. Fellow members included Mary Joslin, Ivy Birch, Maureen Everett, Betty Shelley and Betty Ringer, who marched with me in the Victory parade in 1945.

Jean Johnson

A Happle or a Horange

I had a job on Saturday mornings working for my grandmother. She kept hens and I had to deliver the eggs. I went to a lady in Church Street called Mrs Warren and she would send me to Mrs White opposite. Mrs White would say, 'Would you like a happle or a horange?'

Dennis Johnson

Peeping Toms

We had good times up at Cuppers Farm. The other children and I used to watch from an attic window all the courting couples who spent time under the railway arch. The next day we would pick up sixpences, shillings and even brooches that they had dropped.

Hilda Pluck

Festival of Britain

In 1951 to celebrate the Festival of Britain we had our first carnival in Witham. My friends and I made outfits out of crêpe paper, which had just come in. One of us went as the 'Spirit of the Festival' and used adverts from *Spangles* as sweets were at long last back on the market. Another went as a 'Flower Girl' and I went as a 'Hawaiian Girl'. We put a lot of effort into it and used to sit down every evening and sew our costumes. We went to the starting point in Cressing Road and as Anna took a big step all her stitches came undone. Fortunately some kind lady pinned it back up and we all had a good day.

Shirley Harper

Shirley Harper celebrating the Festival of Britain.

Old Tombstones

As children we often walked round the church graveyard. We were very respectful and took care never to walk on or touch any of the graves. We found the old headstones fascinating and would read the inscriptions with great interest.

Angela Dursley

Twelve-bore Guns

In Witham most farmers had twelve-bore guns; the .22 was a smaller shot for killing rabbits or foxes. We needed to have a licence which was obtained from the post office. I think a lot of the poachers had guns as well. There has always been poachers, hasn't there? Although, saying

that, we farmed fifteen acres and I don't think we had much trouble with them.

Fred Gaymer

Bone Horn

Mr Lawrence from The Grove used to sit in the church in a front pew. He held a big bone horn to his ear so he could hear the sermon.

Bert Baxter

Flick of the Cape

Policemen wore capes over their shoulders and if you misbehaved they flicked their cape at your face or ears – it really hurt.

Dennis Johnson

Holy Family Church

I was born in 1936 and mine was the first baptism in eighteen months at Holy Family church. It was a small parish then and Father Laughton was the parish priest.

Pat Gillen

Eggs to the Farmer

I also took eggs to Mrs Brown who lived at Cocks Farm on the corner of Chalks Road and Braintree Road where the garage is now. I thought it odd taking eggs to a farm, but I think it was mostly arable. For my labours on a Saturday morning I earned fourpence from my grandmother.

Dennis Johnson

Flapping Hair

There was a high-brow concert at the Public Hall which we were strongly encouraged by Miss Croxall to attend. I went and it was boring until the soprano, who wore bangs, reached the high notes. Her hair flapped up and down with the notes and we couldn't stop laughing. Some sneak went back and told Miss Croxall and of course we were in trouble once again.

Jean Johnson

Mr Griggs

Mr Griggs, a local commercial artist who lived in Maldon Road, taught me the rudiments of painting when I wasa young man. It's been a lifetime's hobby. I paint in oils and although I've never pushed it I have actually sold quite a few.

John Hollick

Used Uniforms

Special constables tended to be issued with used uniforms, although regular officers had tailor-made ones with smart blue shirts and detachable collars.

Maureen Scollan

Wasps' Nest

When I should have been at Sunday school I went tree-climbing in Mill Lane with my

George and Cecilia Smith at Rickstones Road.

125

friend Teresa Harrington. She fell inside a tree and disturbed a wasps' nest. The angry wasps followed us all down Mill Lane. Mrs Oakie Claydon came out of her cottage and stripped the screaming Teresa before covering her with a blue bag. I just ran home.

Hilda Pluck

The Peculiar People

From early this century until the fifties my grandparents lived in Rickstones Road. My grandfather, George Smith, was a preacher in the 'Peculiar People'. He preached at the chapel in Guithavon Valley and travelled to other chapels in the area to preach. My grandmother Cecilia was a member of the Horsnell family.

Diane Watson

Bethel Seats

The things I remember when I was young are varied. When I first went to Bethel we had cinema seats because these were all they could get during the war. I played in the meadows a little bit up from Ebenezer Close and swam at Wolseys Corner – the river was deeper there. A friend and I used to cycle to the Whitehall Cinema; we left our bikes in the cycle shed at the back. The prices of the seats then were 1s, 1s 6d or 2s 6d. I normally went in the 1s 6d and I can remember one particular film, a Saturday matinée that we liked very much: it was called *Lorna Doone*. My father enjoyed fishing – we had skate for breakfast, dinner and tea. He fished at Brightlingsea and would often take the ferry boat across the bay to Point Clear.

Pat Taylor

Honest John Strutt

I remember 'Honest John' Strutt. He was a member of the Rayleigh family and my father worked for him on the land. I didn't vote for him as I have always supported the Labour Party. If you were poor like us that was the only way to try and improve things.

Percy Adams

Albert Gaymer in uniform.

Autograph Book

I had a little autograph book which friends and relatives signed or wrote rhymes in. Most little girls liked to have one.

Vera Howell

An Old Card

I remember Miss Hunt: every Easter she would open her doors to the local children. She had a very big table on which were spread all the greetings cards she had received in the past. Miss Hunt would allow us to choose one of her old cards as her Easter gift to us.

Albert Poulter

Volunteer Frontiersmen

I remember the Volunteer Frontiersmen was a good drinking club. They dressed in breeches and scouts' hats, some were on horseback. The chap who lived up Earlsmead used to be in charge. In a way they were like a private police force as they were employed to check that everything was all right around Witham.

Percy Adams

General Anders

There was a large contingent of Polish and Ukrainian men in Witham who had served in the Middle East with the Polish Corps. I worked with them for a while and remember in 1947 or '48 General Anders

Albert Gaymer, aged ninety years.

came to Witham station on his way to visit them.

Pat Smith

Pension

When the Act came in, everyone over eighty-six got a pension. My father drew his pension for the first time on his ninetieth birthday – of course, I did all his correspondence for him.

Fred Gaymer

Holy Family

I got married in the Holy Family church, the old Catholic church. The parish priest at that time was Father Laughton, who was so deaf he had to use a big black hearing horn.

Hilda Pluck

Jellied Eels

When I caught eels, I ate them fried or jellied. If fried I skinned them first; if jellied I left the skin on, boiled them and let them cool until the liquid turned to jelly. I once

Matthew and Daniel Tiller at the Flume.

caught a two-pounder and it lasted me for two or three days.

Ken Smith

No Games on Sundays

On Sundays children were not allowed to play games and had to be quiet. We were certainly not allowed to spend money on sweets or anything else, although I don't think many shops opened on Sundays then.

Vera Howell

Mrs Shoot

I was nineteen years old when I got married to Pete at the United Reformed church. My sister Jane was my bridesmaid and a local lady, Mrs Shoot, made my wedding dress. Our reception was at the White Hart; Pete and I then hired a car and drove to Cheddar Gorge for our honeymoon. That was the first holiday I can remember having; later on we had the caravan at Jaywick.

Margaret Brannan

The Flume

Guithavon Road always got flooded before they put in the Flume to ease the flow of water. This solved the problem, as I can't remember it flooding since. The side of the riverbank by the flume was used as a corporation dump during the war but now is part of the River Walk.

Fred Willshire